STUDIES

OF THE

OLD TESTAMENT.

BY

AUSTIN PHELPS, D.D.,

PROFESSOR AT ANDOVER THEOLOGICAL SEMINARY.
AUTHOR OF "THE STILL HOUR," ETC.

SOLID GROUND CHRISTIAN BOOKS
BIRMINGHAM, ALABAMA USA

Solid Ground Christian Books
PO Box 660132
Vestavia Hills AL 35266
205-443-0311
mike.sgcb@gmail.com
www.solid-ground-books.com

STUDIES OF THE OLD TESTAMENT
Classic Essays to Show the Perpetuity of the Old Testament as a Living Book for All Ages
by Austin Phelps (1820-1890)

First Solid Ground Edition – June 2015

Cover photo from painting *Daniel in the Lions' Den* by Briton Riviere (1840 - 1920)
Cover design by Borgo Design
Contact them at borgogirl@bellsouth.net

ISBN- 978-159925-351-0

INTRODUCTORY NOTE.

THESE studies of the Old Testament were originally published in one of our most widely-circulated religious papers. So many persons have expressed a wish for them in a more permanent form, that they are now gathered into this volume. Slight changes have been made, — a change in the order of topics, an occasional enlargement or alteration of paragraphs, and a few corrections. If the volume serves to illustrate, in any degree, how ancient and neglected Scriptures may be revived in the popular interest, and thus to show the perpetuity of the Old Testament as a *living* book for all ages, the object of this republication will be accomplished.

THEOLOGICAL SEMINARY, ANDOVER, MASS.
Oct. 1, 1878.

CONTENTS.

		PAGE
I.	THE PROPHET OF THE BROKEN HEART	7
II.	GOD WORKS WITH MINORITIES WHO ARE WORKING FOR HIM	21
III.	A MODEL OF PRAYER IN EMERGENCIES	33
IV.	AN ANCIENT REVIVAL OF RELIGION	43
V.	CHRISTIAN ALLIANCES WITH WICKED MEN	55
VI.	HONORING GOD'S HOUSE	67
VII.	PRESUMPTION IN THE WORSHIP OF GOD	79
VIII.	FIDELITY TO THE RELIGION OF A GODLY ANCESTRY	89
IX.	THE LOST SON OF A GODLY FATHER	100
X.	THE GODLY SON OF AN UNGODLY FATHER	111
XI.	THE PRODIGAL SON OF GODLY PARENTS	124
XII.	THE TWIN SERPENTS	137
XIII.	AVOWED ENEMIES OF RELIGION	147
XIV.	A TALK WITH YOUNG PEOPLE ABOUT JOSIAH	161
XV.	AN ANCIENT MODEL OF YOUTHFUL TEMPERANCE	174
XVI.	THE LOST BIBLE	187
XVII.	GOOD MEN WHO ARE NOT CHURCHMEN	201
XVIII.	INTERTWINING OF GOD'S PLANS WITH THE PLANS OF MEN	215
XIX.	THE KINGDOMS THAT DIE, AND THE KINGDOM THAT LIVES	230
XX.	FRUITLESS CONVICTIONS OF SIN	244

CONTENTS.

		PAGE
XXI.	THE MEN IN THE FIRE	261
XXII.	THE MAN IN THE LIONS' DEN	277
XXIII.	THE FULFILMENT OF PROPHECY IN THE CAREER OF CYRUS	295
XXIV.	CHRIST THE CENTRE OF BIBLICAL THOUGHT	314

STUDIES OF THE OLD TESTAMENT.

THE PROPHET OF THE BROKEN HEART.

Oh that my head were waters, and mine eyes a fountain of tears, that I might weep day and night for the slain of the daughter of my people! — JER. ix. 1.

THE "Weeping Prophet" is the title often given to Jeremiah. He is not a popular prophet. Unhappy men are not commonly popular men. Yet this one had ample reason for the depression under which he lived, and the minor key which runs through the strain of his writings. He was very far from being a morose man. He did not mourn over disappointed ambitions of his youth. He was not soured at the world's injustice. He wasted no melodrama over the "cold, cold world." He was the last man living to be a misanthrope.

It may help us to appreciate two of the most affecting and sublime books of the Bible, to inquire, What was it that made this very able and godly man so miserable? Why should he, more than other men, be given over to lifelong sorrow? Why should he, more than other men, leave us a book of "Lamentations" as the most significant record of his life? Why should his name have coined a word, "jeremiad," expressive of the lugubrious and dismal in literature?

The answer is this. He had a most delicately sensitive nature, a most profound attachment to the cause of God, an intense patriotic love of his native land; yet it was his lot to live at an age when the people of God had fallen into most fearful apostasy, and the most terrific judgments were impending over them. It was given to him to see those judgments hurrying on apace. He heard angels of retribution on the wings of the wind. He saw their sabres flashing in the sun.

Moreover, it was his mission to tell the people of their sins, to rebuke the nobles for their oppression, the humbler orders for their vileness, the priesthood for their falseness, even his fellow-prophets for their infidelity to the living God. The whole nation, from prince to beggar, had reached the very bottom of national depravity; and this lone man was set to tell them of it, and to forewarn them of the frightful doom which was impending. He was the prophet of unwelcome truth. He had to face the facts of an age of retribution. He had to tear away the illusions with which people were deceiving themselves. They were bragging of the recovery of the Bible, which Josiah had found in the rubbish of their desecrated temple. They claimed that that sacred treasure was going to make all things right with them. They treated it much as an African savage regards the fetich which he worships, or the amulet which he wears around his neck. The possession of the Sacred Book, they thought, would save them. This young prophet knew better, and he had to tell them so.

The recovered Bible had come too late to save them, just as Christianity now comes to some savage tribes too late to save them from extermination. The people did not want to hear his story. He was a croaker. They wanted to hear somebody who would give them a pleasanter discourse. People who are living in sin, and who know it, are sometimes very fond of "beautiful sermons." They will bear any thing better than the simple truth. Beauty is more popular than truth.

Besides, this unpopular preacher stood alone. Not another one of the prophetic order stood by him. The only friend he had was one Baruch, an obscure scribe; and even he got sadly frightened at the plain talk of his outspoken friend. The priests, too, hated him as a renegade. All classes — some for one reason, and some for another — agreed in their spite against this solitary truth-teller. Like Bunyan and many another unpalatable preacher, he got himself into prison for his fidelity. For forty years it was his business to deliver his warnings and rebukes and threatenings, word for word, as God bade him, to nobles and priests and people who were bent on destruction, and determined not to be saved by God or man.

To him belongs the distinction of first suffering the burning of the word of God by the enraged king who would not listen to his reproofs. Many times after his day, faithful preachers and reformers saw the Bible burned in the market-place by royal and papal decree. But the first in the long line of such honored men was this despondent prophet of Judæa. On him Satan first wreaked that form of impotent revenge. As if a truth could be burned with a flaming scroll!

A singular fact also is it, that this solitary preacher, the butt of a nation's ridicule, does not seem to have been made for such work. Usually God fits the man to his life's work. If he is to have stern work to do, he is made of stern stuff. Luther, with much that was lovable in his nature, was, on the whole, a rough, stout man. That square face and thick neck, and those compact lips of his, indicate a man of will, who could bear rougher handling than other men. He was to contend with devils; and God gave him a nature which devils feared. Nobody ever called Luther the "weeping prophet." If he shed tears, it was on his knees before God only. He shed no tears

THE PROPHET OF THE BROKEN HEART. 11

before the Diet of Worms. He was in no lachrymose mood when he had the pope's bull to deal with, outside the Elster Gate of Wittenberg.

The mourning prophet of Judæa does not seem to have been of that stern make. He had a delicate and retiring nature. Gentle and unselfish was he, like a loving woman. When the sombre truth first dawns upon his early manhood, and he sees the work he has to do, he breaks out with the despairing cry, "Ah, Lord! I cannot speak! I am but a child!" So overwhelmed is he by the sight of his country's shame, and the foresight of her doom, that he exclaims, "Oh that my head were waters, that I might weep day and night for the daughter of my people!" His writings show, by their chosen imagery, that he longs for solitude. He hungers to get away from the sins and sorrows of his time. Cowper's refrain, "Oh for a lodge in some vast wilderness!" would have expressed the habit of his mind. He "sits alone, and keeps silence, crouching under his burden." We seem to hear him crying out in the bitterness of his spirit, —

"The time is out of joint. Oh, cursed spite,
That ever I was born to set it right!"

It is very significant of the despair of his soul, that he lives a celibate life. It is not for such a man as he to seek the dear delights of family and companionships of home. His great life's work is too sad, too heart-breaking. He will not venture to lay the half of it on the heart of any woman. At times, when the solitude of it, and the blackness of it, and the funeral dirge of it, become intolerable, he heaps curses on the day of his birth. True to his Oriental instincts, he curses the very messenger who bore the glad news to his father that a boy was born to bear his name. Yes, he is the Prophet of the Broken Heart. The sins of his people are a lifelong grief to him. His own work, as their spiritual teacher, overwhelms him. The mystery of his life is, why he, of all men living, should have been called to such a mission, among such a people, on the eve of their destruction, too late to do them any good; when all that he can do is to proclaim to them the judgments with which they are soon to be overtaken.

When the late Rev. Charles Kingsley was in his last sickness, and very near his end, though he did not know it, but was waiting in anguish for the daily expected death of his wife, he said one day, as his biographer tells us, "It must be right; for it is so *strange* and yet so painful." The very mysteriousness of inexplicable trial is a token of the divine wisdom from which it comes. No other mind could contrive trial so profound. It must come from God, and "must be right." Such was the forlorn consolation of the stricken prophet, when overwhelmed, as he often was, by the lot which it had pleased God to send him. Even

God's veracity he questions: "O Lord, thou hast deceived me, and I was deceived." Imprecations flow from his lips like household words.

To his own times and people he was the prophet of doom. So far as they were concerned, his work ended there. Not so in the fore-reaching design of God. Jeremiah "builded better than he knew." He did an unconscious work for coming ages. Imperfect man as he was, he was the forerunner of the *spiritual* disclosures of the new dispensation. The old dispensation was near its end. Its sun was going down in blood-red clouds. But the spiritual meaning of the ancient forms and rites was coming slowly to the light. To no other prophet of the olden time, unless it be Isaiah, do we turn for glimpses of it as we do to this despairing one. The very burden of his soul pressed it out of him. He was driven to fall back upon the spiritual truths and consolations which his own soul needed. His very sins made them a necessity to him. Nothing else could save him from mania or suicide. God thus *used* him, his sorrows, his self-conflicts, his errors, his sins.

Let us pass rapidly over a few suggestions drawn from this sketch of this remarkable man: —

1. Jeremiah *represents a class of good men and women* of whom some exist in every age. There are some good men of whom it must be conceded that they are not gay Christians. From their make, and from the disclosures of truth which

God gives them, they cannot be. They have a peculiarly sensitive and deep nature. They have profound intuitions. Their religion is proportionately deep and tender. In all this world's history, nothing else is so startling a *fact* to them as that this is a lost world, estranged from God, on its way, but for God's loving grace, to an eternal and awful doom.

These men and women are often blamed for being gloomy. In their hearts they answer, "How can we be hilarious when the imperilled souls of men, and our own too, rest as a burden upon us?" If the world were enveloped in one vast conflagration, should we naturally laugh and sing and dance our way through it? Yet a more fearful flame is ravaging it than that of the fires of Etna. A certain sobriety of deportment seems to such men becoming to life in such a world as this, and with such a future crowding on its destiny.

Christian ministers, whose work compels them to think much of these things, are apt to be so oppressed by them as to acquire a certain gravity of demeanor which the world laughs at. If you could look into their hearts, as you sometimes do in their memoirs, you would see that they bear the burden day and night of this *lost* world.

2. Christians of the broken heart, it must be confessed, *are not apt to be popular with the world.* Very hard things are said of them. Very unjust judgments they have to bear in silence. The world

cracks many a jest upon their long faces and their "vinegar" aspect. I have seen tears trembling in their eyes, as their only answer to the gibes of men for whose souls they went home to pray.

Yet have not you heard from such jesters the fling at our common faith, "If I believed what you believe, I should move heaven and earth to save souls: it seems to me I could never laugh again"? So said an estimable woman of the world to me last summer. It is hard to please men who do not feel the inner life which many humble Christians lead. Which shall we do, gentlemen and ladies, which shall we do?—hold on to, and try to act upon, the faith that gives us "long faces," or meet your charge of heartless inconsistency by living as if this were already a saved world, and our home were Eden?

3. The class of godly men and women of whom Jeremiah is the type *possess a very profound style of Christian character*. Not perfect, by any means. We all have an ideal of a certain robust and rounded Christian life superior to theirs. On the whole, St. Paul was a nobler character then Jeremiah. He ought to have been. He saw at its meridian the sun which the prophet only *foresaw* long before the dawn. Yet it is unjust not to give the Jeremiahs of our brotherhood the credit for ploughing deep in their sense of eternal things. They may not be as happy as their faith in Christ warrants them to be. Yet they do make a begin-

ning in the right direction. Theirs is a *struggle* to be and to do, of which they have no reason to be ashamed. They do not cover their eyes. They accept God's teachings courageously. Eternity will show to us all, that some of the world's *great souls* are among them. Multitudes who were more popular with their fellow-men here will there stand aside, and leave a clear space for those mourning ones to go up and hear God's message to them. Does anybody doubt what that will be?

4. Such Christians as the "weeping prophet" represents *are men and women of great spiritual power.* The world does not like them, but cannot help respecting them. "I keep clear of unhappy people," said one of the impatient ones: yet I observed that he chose for his pastor, and honored as a great man, one whose face was long, and whose look betokened secret tears. We love realities, after all. We feel the power of the man who knows the most of them, and feels them most profoundly. The man or woman who takes God's view of things, interprets human life as God interprets it, looks out on eternity as God reveals it, and whose visage bears the marks of inward struggles of soul with the facts of human destiny as God declares them, is a *power* with us all. If we come into deep waters, and the billows go over our heads, we look around grasping for the friendly word or look or hand of such to cheer us. The very men we have laughed at, or shrunk from,

because they were "unco' guid men," are those whose experience we want then.

Said one man of the world, whose misfortune it was to have a "gay parson" for his pastor, "Our pastor is a capital fellow, a born wit, a splendid mimic; he keeps the table in a roar; and in the pulpit he is not afraid to make us laugh." Said his friend, "Suppose that you had lost your only child, or that you were yourself about to die." — "Well," was the reply, "to tell you the truth, he is the last man I should want to see then. Still he is a capital fellow."

Somehow the "capital fellows," in the ministry or out of it, are a little limited in their range of usefulness. They do for picnics or the croquet-ground. When we come to those passages of life or death at which eternity looks in upon us, we turn to men and women of another make.

5. Who can help seeing that broken-hearted Christians *are in some respects very nearly akin to the Lord Jesus Christ?*

Does not their life, dropping its inconsistencies, strike us very much as his life does? He did not live a very hilarious life. Jests are not the chief thing we remember from his lips. His biographers do not say much of his "eyes sparkling with fun," and his "ringing laugh." He was never called a "capital fellow." Such clergymen as Matthew Byles and Sydney Smith, somehow, do not remind us very impressively of him. He attended a wedding; but the chief thing he did there had more to do with eternity than with time, more to do with God than with man. Comic songs — But stop! Let us take off our shoes from our feet, for the ground whereon we stand is holy!

The sorrows of men had a strange attraction for him. He did not "keep clear of unhappy men." The grave of Lazarus was the scene of one of the events most strikingly *like* him. The way he felt about Jerusalem seems very much like that of the weeping prophet. The nights he spent in prayer are a great comfort to these Christians of the broken heart. Of Gethsemane and Calvary what shall we say? May we reverently ask what class of Christians most nearly resemble him there? What kind of disciples did he long to see around him then? What is the meaning of that prophetic portrait of him which painters have never copied, "His visage was marred more than any man, and his form more than the sons of men"?

6. Let us not be misunderstood. It is not that the example even of the "Man of Sorrows" forbids mirth, the laugh, the song, the jest. No: there is a time to laugh, and a time to dance. Rejoice, O young man, in thy youth, and let thy heart cheer thee! Christ never by one word or look enjoined ascetic virtues. He lived so that bad men called him a glutton. Men who prayed in the streets with one eye open called him a winebibber. Men who cheated widows said he was a

sabbath-breaker. Adulterers charged him with unseemly acquaintance with outcast women. Murderers and blasphemers called him the devil. He was no saint according to the standard of such men. Nevertheless, the whole drift of his teachings and his life was towards a different *kind* of life from that which men call pleasure. Its joys lie deeper, and are built upon certain august and stern realities. And those realities it is which these Christians of the downcast eye are struggling with, some of them, day by day, all their lives long.

We do them a very mean injustice if we fail to give them credit for this. They are simply struggling, like drowning men, as for dear life, to be true to the faith they hold. With heavy hearts and swollen eyes, they are trying to *live* their faith. They are agonizing to get near to Christ, and to live there. Drowning men do not sing many comic songs. Ye cynical critics, think what you may of the rest of us: there *are* such men and women as these, of whom Christ is not ashamed. Oh, what poor fools we are if we profane their conflicts with a gibe!

7. These Christians of the broken heart *are sure of a very exalted rank in heaven.* I hear a voice from beyond the stars, saying, "Blessed are they that mourn, for they shall be comforted. Blessed are they that hunger and thirst after righteousness, for they shall be filled. What are these that are

arrayed in white robes? Whence came they? These are they that came out of great tribulation: *therefore* are they before the throne of God, and serve him day and night in his temple. They shall hunger no more, neither thirst any more: and God shall wipe away all tears from their eyes."

GOD WORKS WITH MINORITIES WHO ARE WORKING FOR HIM.

Be not afraid nor dismayed by reason of this great multitude; for the battle is not yours, but God's. . . . Ye shall not need to fight: . . . stand ye still, and see the salvation of the Lord: . . . fear not, the Lord will be with you. — 2 CHRON. xx. 15, 17.

AT the darkest hour of our civil war, when the life of the country seemed trembling in the balance, the Government proclaimed a fast. The people gathered in immense numbers in the churches. Men not often seen there were found there on that day. An eminent civilian in one of our Atlantic cities, who seldom sought God's house on the Lord's Day, was observed on that fast day kneeling devoutly with God's people. When inquired of what brought *him* out to such services, he replied, "I thought it was high time to get *help* somewhere. We are in a tight place, and we need it."

Men often seek God in "a tight place," when they think little of him in other places. It is marvellous how reasonable and proper *prayer* seems to them in such emergencies.

Such was the condition of the Judæan kingdom

at the time of which our text speaks. A fast had just been observed; the entire people had come together to obtain help of God "in a tight place." He gave them their desire, as he commonly does when men in trouble turn to him for relief. And in giving it he announced one of the great principles of his working in the affairs of his kingdom: *he works with minorities who are working for him.* "Be not afraid nor dismayed by reason of this great multitude; for the battle is not yours, but God's." Go out against them. The Lord will be with you.

1. The history of the Church is full of illustrations of this law of divine procedure. Dip into it anywhere, and you come upon this divine strategy. Napoleon thought that he knew the world well. He had studied the history of great empires; but he said it was an inexplicable mystery to him, that Christianity, beginning as it did with a few fishermen of the feeblest nation then on the globe, should in his time have risen to be so much more mighty than his own conquests, which had almost all the armies of Europe to back them.

> "Oh! where are kings and empires now,
>   Of old that went and came?
> But, Lord, thy Church is praying yet,
>   A thousand years the same."

It was God's way of working with minorities who are working for him. When the Church became corrupt, and needed reform, the same thing was repeated. A few earnest men, who were hunted like wild beasts, in a few years shook the world. The battle was not theirs, but God's.

An old saying of the German reformers, which a modern reformer has untruthfully claimed as his own, was, "One, with God on his side, is a majority." "The battle is not yours, but God's." This fragment of our lesson was the favorite text of Sir Fowell Buxton. He once wrote to his daughter that she would find his Bible opening of itself to the place where this passage occurs. This text it was which gave him courage to move in the British Parliament for the emancipation of slaves throughout the British Empire. When he entered on that conflict, he stood almost alone; when his bill was first read in Parliament, it was received with shouts of derisive laughter. But he bethought him of this text, and began his speech saying, "Mr. Speaker, the reading of this bill is the beginning of a movement which will surely end in the abolition of slavery throughout the British dominions." The old Hebrew prophet never said a truer word. Sir Fowell knew it; for the battle was not his, but God's.

The same phenomenon was witnessed in the first attempt to establish American missions among the heathen. When one of the early meetings of the American Board was held at Bradford, Mass., less than twenty persons were in attendance; and they were hooted at by boys on the piazza of the hotel where they were in session. Barely sixty-five years have passed; and at the last meeting of that Board, in Providence, five thousand strangers from abroad were present, and two churches were filled with eager friends.

When the first American missionaries reached India, the English Government refused them a landing. "Go back," was the imperious order: "go back in the ship in which you came." In the General Assembly of the Church of Scotland, when it was first proposed to send the gospel to the heathen, reverend clergymen declared against the fanatical scheme. They said that "the heathen were a contented and happy people, and that it was no business of Scottish Christians to disturb them." And this in face of our Lord's express command, "Go ye into all the world, and preach the gospel to every creature." Not a century has passed since that time: yet now all Christendom rings with gratulation over the achievement of Christian missions; and no other class of men are so reverently canonized in the affections of the Church as her missionaries to the heathen world. This is the fruit of God's working with minorities who are working for him.

So uniform has been this method of divine procedure, that we may safely say that great progress of any good cause is seldom if ever secured in any other way. When a good cause becomes popular, and majorities swing over to its support, the work is substantially done. Probably some new cause is then coming to the birth underneath. Every cause which God originates starts with only Gideon's three hundred.

2. From this law of God's working, it is clear that *in spiritual affairs the balance of power does not depend on numbers.* Votes have very little to do with it. It depends on spiritual forces. It depends on insight into the spiritual wants of the world; on consecration to God's service; on the power of prayer; on spiritual discovery of the side on which God is; and specially on *intensity* of Christian character.

The few who start a great movement towards the world's conversion, and who become its heroes because God has chosen them, are always *intense* men. They see things vividly. They have great visions. They feel profoundly. Their souls are aflame with holy ardor. "His ministers are a flaming fire." Yet they are men of *sustained* enthusiasm. The fire does not crackle and blaze out quickly: it burns like kindled anthracite. In the best sense they are men of one idea, — a vast idea, in which a thousand common ones are centred, yet *one* to which whole souls can be reasonably devoted. So far as this world is concerned, God is possessed of one idea.

Such men are always a power in the world. The world cannot help it, and they cannot help it.

Such men are one of God's powers, imperial in authority, and destined to conquest. In due time numbers will swell around them. Meanwhile it is of very little account how many or how few they are at the outset.

> "A little flock: so calls He thee
> Who bought thee with his blood;
> A little flock, disowned of men,
> But owned and loved of God."

3. It is a great thought on this subject, that *the human race furnishes but a small part of the holy ministries of this world*. The ministry of angels probably swells what we call minorities to secret majorities. "Are they not *all* ministering spirits?" Invisible multitudes probably fill the air with their busy pinions in service to the right. We are surrounded with a great cloud of witnesses. When conflicts deepen on the earth, for and against the cause of Christ, other worlds send hosts of eager combatants to the fray. Probably no child of God is ever left without these unseen auxiliaries. "He shall give his angels charge over *thee*." Earthly monarchs often form secret treaties of alliance, offensive and defensive, by which each pledges the whole force of his kingdom to the support of the other. Let us have faith to see the unseen, and it may often help our wavering courage to remember that countless myriads are in secret alliance with us.

One of England's great poets says of a noted champion of liberty, —

> " Thou hast left behind
> Powers that will work for thee; air, earth, and skies:
> There's not a breathing of the common wind
> That will forget thee. Thou hast great allies.
> . . . Winds blow and waters roll
> Strength to the brave."

But the friend of Christ has allies more imperial than skies and winds and waters. Principalities in heavenly places, beings some of whom probably sway at their will the powers of nature, are his allies.

4. *Success in spiritual affairs often loses the character of a conflict*, so overwhelming and so easy is the working of divine auxiliaries. Thus ran the good cheer to the outnumbered men of Judah: " Ye shall not need to fight in this battle: stand ye still, and see the salvation of the Lord with you." God's help often comes in immense waves of spiritual re-enforcements. Our small calculations and petty fears are overborne. We are lifted up, and carried over the obstacles which daunted us. We can no longer find the perils which alarmed us. This comes about with such ease and stillness that we lose the sense of struggle and of combat.

Revivals of religion often take on this look. The more powerful and pure they are, the more still and godlike. At such periods sanguine be-

lievers are apt to think the age of conflict for the
Church is over, and the latter days of peace and
tranquil progress are dawning. In the great
awakenings in New England, under the preaching
of the Rev. Drs. Lyman Beecher and Nettleton, it
was a favorite theme of gratulation to them, that
probably the closing age of this world's pilgrimage
was near at hand, and the golden visions of Isaiah
were about to be realized. They seemed to themselves to stand still, and see the salvation of the
Lord.

5. *Minorities of honest and earnest men, devoted
to a great cause, should never be opposed heedlessly.*
If it is God's method to begin great changes for
good by putting into the hearts of a few men
great ideas and great enterprises and great expectation, we need to be cautious how we treat men
who *may be* spiritual pioneers. It is the way of
the world to frown them down. They are branded
with scornful nicknames. Fanatics, madmen,
fools, men call them. "The crazy tinker" was
the title by which the world labelled and libelled
the author of the "Pilgrim's Progress." "Methodists," "Puritans," "Quakers," — all nicknames at
first. Not so will the wise and candid treat such
men.

Fanaticism may always be detected by its affinity
with malign passions. Religious earnestness is not
fanaticism. Novelty in religious thought and
theory of life is not presumptively visionary.

GOD WORKS WITH MINORITIES. 29

That men turn the world upside down, is no proof that they are madmen. St. Paul did that. When men are obviously moved by profound convictions, and are in dead earnest in proclaiming them, if they are honest, candid, prayerful, unselfish men, and do not contradict either the word of God or the common sense of men, they deserve a hearing. They *may be* heralds of a new era of Christian progress. Their ideas *may be* from God. The power which moves them *may be* the power of God. Their self-confidence *may be* a divine assurance, prophetic of the future. "The homely beauty of the good *old* cause" may be about to spring into new life and glory in their hands.

Take care that you do not recklessly denounce and deride such men, lest you should denounce and deride God. It is like God to raise up such men, and inspire them, and send them to his people, as he sent the old prophets. A docile spirit will welcome God's teaching, come in what form it may. God usually sends in forms which men have not expected. The true attitude of a Christian thinker and worker toward such phenomena is one of vigilance and candor. Wisdom did not die with our fathers; neither will it die with us. Old men will not carry it out of the world with them. New truth must be expected from new men. The world has yet to see a great many John the Baptists, voices in the wilderness, forerunners of great eras.

Let us, then, be on the lookout for such men. Let us greet them with a God-speed when they make their divine credentials clear. Let us keep our *tastes* in abeyance to our *convictions*. We love what we are used to. We revere the ancient. We all have roots in the venerable past. This is well. Yet the grandest arena of God's working is the future. A Christian's treasure should be there. Ours is a religion of hope, of expectation, of onlooking to golden ages yet to come. Blessed were those Jews in our Lord's time who stood *waiting* for his coming, ready to receive him with open hearts. Blessed, too, are the *foreseeing* men and women of all ages, who are always watching for the morning; praying for great things; working for great things; expecting great things; bending forward, and listening for the prophetic voices; quick to see the great light in the heavens, when it first gilds the tops of the eastern hills.

6. *Within the Church of Christ itself is to be found a minority of believers whom God regards with peculiar complacency.* An eminent clergyman of Philadelphia once expressed the opinion that a majority of the professed followers of Christ do not add any *appreciable* strength to the spiritual power of the Church. It saddens one to think that this may be true. Be it true or not, the fact cannot be doubted that there is within the Church a body of believers of peculiar spirituality of character and consistency of life, who are generally a minority.

There is a church within the Church. St. John in his vision of the future declares, "Blessed and holy is he that hath part in the *first* resurrection. They shall be kings and priests unto God, and shall reign with him a thousand years." Whatever that may mean, it implies *gradation* in the spiritual rank of the redeemed. This tallies with what we see in the Church on earth. There are Christians who always live near to God. They are obviously bent on living as Christ lived. They live as if they belonged to God. Their property they treat as his, not their own. They are always ready for Christian work. A revival of religion never takes them by surprise. They live in a revival perpetually. They are men and women of much prayer. Pastors depend upon them in emergencies, as they cannot upon all professed believers. We always know where to find them, and never find them in the wrong place, on the wrong side, saying the wrong word, doing the wrong thing.

Theirs is not a religion of form, not a religion of intermittent and erratic feeling, not a religion of æsthetic taste, but a religion of deep and controlling principle. As a spiritual power, they are the vanguard of the Church. They are the spiritual aristocracy of Christ's kingdom. These are they who shall sit on his right hand and on his left without asking for the dignity. Princes are they in prayer, conquerors in conflict with the powers of evil, saints to whom the truculent criticism of the world even does not refuse the title.

Almost every large church contains a group of such Christians, few or more, yet commonly a minority. Sometimes they can be numbered on one's fingers. "I have *one* man in my church," said an aged pastor not long ago, — "I have *one* man on whom I can always depend. I do not know that I have another." It is a legitimate object of prayer and Christian aspiration, to be numbered among those chosen few. God looks upon them with complacent joy. Christ sees in them of the travail of his soul. They satisfy him. Like David, they are men after God's own heart. Like John, they are beloved disciples. Like Mary, they have chosen the good part. Like Paul, they fight a good fight. Their very presence in the world, the world feels as a power on the side of right. Every good cause feels the loss of them when they die. As we stand beside their open graves, we thank God anew for the doctrine of immortality. One star differeth from another star in glory. So also is the resurrection of the dead.

A MODEL OF PRAYER IN EMERGENCIES.

And Asa cried unto the Lord his God, and said, Lord, it is nothing with thee to help, whether with many, or with them that have no power: help us, O Lord our God; for we rest on thee, and in thy name we go against this multitude. O Lord, thou art our God; let not man prevail against thee. —2 CHRON. xiv. 11.

THE prayers recorded in the Bible are almost all of them models in their place. Such is the prayer of the Jewish monarch in the text.

King Asa is in a great strait. To all human appearance, his throne and his life are in peril. His Ethiopian enemy is in battle array before him, with numbers in the proportion to his own of about two to one. His defeat is morally certain. He and his staff must have felt, in that valley of Ephratah, as they looked over the roods of glittering spears, as our own Washington felt in Valley Forge, in the most dismal winter of the Revolution. He seems to himself to have come to the place of extreme catastrophe. He he can only lie down and die.

Like the "Father of his Country," the Jewish king betakes himself to prayer. It is about all there is left for him to do, preliminary to the fatal morrow. His petition is very brief. In great emergencies our wants are summed up in few words. We have no heart for more. This is the *model of prayer in an emergency.* It is made up of four fragments, each of which teaches us a fundamental element in the spirit of prayer in such an exigency.

1. Prayer in emergencies *should be founded on a strong faith in God's independence of human resources and methods of judgment.* Hear the stricken monarch, as he kneels beneath the weight of a kingdom: "Lord, it is nothing to thee to help, whether with many or with them that have no power." This goes to the heart of the case. Nothing else equals the situation. "True," we seem to hear him plucking up his own courage in the extremity, — "true, I am outnumbered. Every man of us must engage two to-morrow. The best military science of the age is pitted against us. These Ethiopian invaders are no mean folk. They are stalwart men, led by able generals, flushed with victories. They are doubtless laughing at our temerity, and glorying in our coming shame. And by all human calculations they are right. They are sure to win: we are doomed to fail. The laws of war bid us make the best terms of peace we can. Now is the time for a masterly retreat. But — No: not so, not so! What are numbers to the God of Judah? What are military tactics, and captains

of renown, and the pomp of conquest, — what are they all to the God of Israel? A small matter, — a very small matter. I remind me of the Red Sea. Our God is the living God. He made the heavens and the earth. The nations are as a drop in a bucket. He taketh up the islands as a very little thing. Yes, Lord, it is nothing to thee to help us in this emergency. It is like thee to give the battle to the weak. It is like thee to overthrow the many by the few."

Military history, in every age, is not destitute of similar occurrences. There have been Christian generals, who, to the world's eye, have seemed to have mysterious successes. They who watched the career of Gen. Havelock in India observed this feature in his history. His superiors used to put him upon service to which they dared not send other men. They said that he often succeeded, where, by the laws of war, he ought not to succeed. Whether due to his habits of prayer, or not, there was the fact.

In our own civil war, on one occasion, the general in command of certain forces broke out with the exclamation, on the eve of battle, "We have got them now, and they know it. God Almighty cannot save them." So he had "got them," by all human reckoning of the chances. His staff responded, "Yes, we are sure of them." But it happened, — how much it had to do with the fortunes of the day, we will not presume to say, but it happened, — that the commander-in-chief on the other side was a praying man. He had that morning spent an hour in his tent, invoking divine interposition in the coming conflict. The close of the day found him again in his tent offering thanksgiving for a victory, while the presumptuous general who thought that " God Almighty could not defeat him " was in ignominious flight down the valley of the Shenandoah.

Why should it not be so? Such men command invisible allies. They invoke the onset of spiritual battalions. They lead their enemies into ambuscades of angelic legions. If our eyes were not holden, we might see that the very air is full of them.

Are there not, in the lives of us all, emergencies in which our deliverance may depend on our realizing to our faith the principle that God is independent of the resources which decide human judgment? In certain extreme hours, very much may depend on the depth of our faith in this. Our own courage may depend on it. Our power to energize others may depend on it. Our power with God may depend on it. We need to feel that prayer may command improbable results, because it commands supernatural resources.

Much is gained also when we appreciate the *ease* with which God achieves marvellous issues in response to prayer. " A God doing wonders " is one of his significant titles, — significant of the

A MODEL OF PRAYER IN EMERGENCIES. 37

usage of his dominion. To him there are no such things as emergencies. Prayer never finds him overwhelmed by surprises.

> "To thee there's nothing old appears, —
> Great God, *there's nothing new.*"

The magnitude of our requests never startles his composure. In his serene life, there are no extreme hours, no critical junctures, no unforeseen contingencies. He is never conscious of an hour when his resources run low, when his powers are put to the strain, when he is weary and would pause to rest. The affairs of the universe are never a burden to him.

Note the biblical way of describing the acts of God: "He *spake*, and it was done. He *commanded*, and it stood fast. God *said*, Let there be light, and there was light." The serenity of the stars characterizes all his working. So calmly, so easily, with such assurance of reserved forces and unused energies, does he perform, in answer to prayer, achievements which overwhelm our puny thought by their magnitude. Armies in the shock of battle he sways as easily as the breathing of an infant.

A few years ago there appeared in our skies the most brilliant comet of the century. It was six millions of miles distant from our globe. Such was the speed of its movement, that, if it had been aimed hither in its march, it would have come crashing upon us in less than two days, with the momentum of a hundred and fifty thousand miles an hour. Yet God held that blazing meteor in its appointed groove, worn by millions of years of travel, so that it glided gently across our world's orbit with motion imperceptible. It had the stillness of a painting. Our infant children looked out upon it, and bade it good-night, as a beautiful plaything in the sky, without so much as the closing of an eyelid at the eternal rush of its progress. So calm, so facile, so beautifully silent, are God's wonder-workings in answer to prayer. Mysteries so vast and so anomalous that astonished angels desire to look into them, occur with the ease of a summer twilight.

We need to believe this. With all our hearts we need to accept it as the natural way of God's procedure. We need to be uplifted on the wings of faith to the divine plane of things in our emergencies. Then we can look *down* upon them as aëronauts above the clouds look down upon thunder-storms and tornadoes, from a region of unutterable stillness and under an unclouded sun.

2. The example before us suggests, as a second element in believing prayer in emergencies, *a profound sense of the inadequacy of all other sources of relief but God*. We need to feel that we are shut in to God, and God only. "Help us, O Lord our God, for we rest in thee." This is the plea of the imperilled monarch. This is his argument for the

A MODEL OF PRAYER IN EMERGENCIES. 39

rescue of his tottering kingdom: "We are helpless. Our forces are outnumbered beyond the reach of human daring. We can die, but we can do no more. By all chances, as men count them, we are doomed. We do not know which way to turn. There is no turning for us. We march right on to death. We are shut up to the arm of God. Help, Lord, or we perish."

This familiar element in the spirit of prayer, emergencies force upon our thought. Often divine Providence seems to second the procedure of divine grace by leaving us in a great emergency till we feel this. Deliverance is slow in coming. Prayer is not answered in a breath. The trial gathers intensity. The crisis deepens. The fire waxes hot. The object seems to be to quicken in the soul the sense of God as a reality because he is felt to be a necessity. Ruin here, ruin there, ruin everywhere except in the one thought that there is a God. Intense conceptions of the reality of God come to some minds in no other way than through this secret alliance of providence and grace in the discipline. The needed convictions have to be burned in by fiery trial.

But when the end is gained, when God becomes an infinite fact, when we become content to go fearless into solitude with God, to cast every thing upon God, to rest in God, then believing prayer wells up sweet and fresh from the heart, and flows out in glad assurance from the lips. Then relief, success, conquest, is not far off.

In this spirit, not only the great exigencies of the Church need to be met, but the emergencies of individual life as well. Said Whitefield in one of the crises of his life, "I have thrown myself blindfold into His almighty arms." Said the late Rev. Dr. Griffin in a similar exigency, "I feel that God is all that is left to me."

Every human life lies through some such valleys of Ephratah, where the man seems to himself shut out from all human sources of support, and shut in to solitude with God. If such crises are met in the spirit of believing prayer, they are the precursors of triumph. Some conquest of opposing forces, or some self-conquest preparative to heaven, or some conquest over powers of darkness of which only God and angels are the witnesses, is in the near future.

3. Prayer in emergencies, as illustrated in the example before us, involves a third element. It is a *profound identification with God.* "In thy name we go against this multitude." That is, "The battle is not ours, but God's. Our interests are lost in God's interests. Selfish desire can have no place here. We are lifted and driven beyond all that. For God we pray; for God we fight."

So Luther felt in the great crisis of his life. "Here stand I for God: I can do no other." So the great leaders of the Church have marched to victory. Until the cause at stake is thus identified with God, prevailing prayer is impossible. In

A MODEL OF PRAYER IN EMERGENCIES. 41

a selfish prayer we beat the winds. Nothing is sure in this world but the purposes of God. No interests are safe but his. No cause is secure but his.

Until we can get our private individual concerns within the lines of his plans, we can be sure of nothing. This is the province of believing prayer in emergencies, — to lift us up and out from our petty selves, and so unite us with God that our interests are his because his interests have become ours. Our will is his because his will has been accepted as ours. Then prayer becomes but a prophecy of his decree. Its success is a foregone conclusion. While we are speaking, the answer is on our own lips. One design, doubtless, of great and crushing emergencies, is to help us up to this summit of identification with God, by driving us up the rocky steep that leads thither.

4. One other phase of prayer in such emergencies, suggested by the fragment of biography before us, is *a hearty recognition of God's ownership of us*. "O Lord, thou art our God; let not man prevail against thee."

To Jewish thought the force of this language was intensified by comparison with pagan theories of Godhead. Every nation was believed to have its deity. Ethiopia had her god, and Judæa had hers. When a Jew therefore said, "Thou art our God," he meant to acknowledge God's ownership of him and all his belongings. That any other nation should prevail against Judæa, meant to Jewish thought a victory of man over the living God.

This gave deep significance to Jewish prayer on the eve of battle. Not only was his cause God's cause, by his being identified with God, but he and all he had belonged to God. His success, therefore, was God's success, and his defeat was God's defeat. "Let not *man* prevail against *Thee!*"

This conception of prayer in critical exigencies fills up the Christian idea of it to the brim. *We belong to God.* Whatever concerns us concerns him. Our sorrow is his sorrow. Our joy is his joy. If it is best for us that we be delivered, it is as much to God as to us that he shall send deliverance. No wedge can be driven between, to separate him from us, his interests from ours. The sacredness and eternity of divine ownership are pledged to our success.

By the right of creation *we belong to God.* By the right of faithful and undying friendship *we belong to God.* By the right of eternal redemption *we belong to God.* By the right of purchase with the blood of Christ *we belong to God.* Will God desert his own with such rights as these?

AN ANCIENT REVIVAL OF RELIGION.

When Asa heard these words, he took courage, and put away the abominable idols out of all the land, . . . and renewed the altar of the Lord. . . . And he gathered all Judah and Benjamin, and the strangers with them: . . . for they fell to him in abundance, when they saw that the Lord his God was with him. . . . And they entered into a covenant to seek the Lord God of their fathers, with all their heart and with all their soul. . . . And they sware unto the Lord with a loud voice, and with shouting, and with trumpets, and with cornets. And all Judah rejoiced at the oath: for they had sworn with all their heart, and sought him with their whole desire; and he was found of them: and the Lord gave them rest round about.— 2 CHRON. xv. 8, 9, 12–15.

REVIVALS are supposed by many to be of modern origin; their opponents say, of modern invention. Not so; for here in the heart of the Old Testament we find a record of a revival which tallies, with singular accuracy, with similar works of divine grace in our own day.

As the narrative runs, there has been a long period of religious decline. Israel has been "without the true God, and without a teaching priest, and without law." The services of religion have been grossly neglected: idolatry has overspread the kingdom. Then trouble comes. As usual, God rebukes irreligion by calamity. War ravages the land. No man's life or property is safe. "God did vex them with all adversity."

In their affliction they turn again to God. "They sought him, and he was found of them." God is never far off from men in trouble. An obscure prophet, nowhere else named in the Scriptures, rouses the king to attempt a general reformation of the people. The king sets to work with a will, and a wide-spread work of divine grace is the result. It is a clear case of deliberate seeking for and working for a revival of religion, and with success.

1. Varying somewhat the order of the narrative, we see first that *the heart of a revival lies in a renewal of the covenant of the Church with God.* "They entered into a covenant to seek the Lord God of their fathers, with all their heart and with all their soul." And again, "They had sworn with all their heart, and sought him with their whole desire." Clearly they mean to make a business of it. It is no half-way affair. With the stern zeal characteristic of a semi-civilized age and a theocratic government, they determine that opposers shall suffer for it. "Whosoever would not seek the Lord should be put to death." Yes, they are evidently in dead earnest. By their theory the whole nation is the Church; and the Church must be purified, cost what it may.

One of the laws of the working of the Holy Spirit is disclosed here. A revival of religion begins in the Church of Christ. Rarely, if ever, does an exception occur. God does not work independently of his chosen people. The conversion of the world waits on the will of the Church.

The history of revivals emphasizes this law. A dead Church holds back from God the dead world. An awakened Church is the pioneer of an awakened world. A fragment of the Church vitalized by the Spirit of God will be felt by a godless community. Godly faith is a great power. It takes but little of it to set men thinking and asking what it means. Apply a little fire, in one small spot, to a block of marble, and you soon send a fissure rending through the whole. So the quickening of one small church by a new infusion of divine grace will break up the solidity of sin through a whole community. A little group of men who mean what they say, and who say the great truths of God and an eternal world, will always get a hearing. Crowds often follow one man who has received a new baptism from on high. There is a wonderful magnetism about such a man.

2. A second feature in this ancient revival of religion was *a public proclamation of a revived faith before the world*. It is often objected to modern revivals, that men make so much ado about them. Religion, it is said, is a still affair. It lies between a man's own soul and God. We are commanded to pray in secret chambers with the door shut.

Why all this noise about living to God and saving souls? Rid us of this cant. Give us rather the poetry of a silent faith. Let each man look after his own soul, and not annoy his neighbors. As one such wise man once expressed it, "Let each man have a snug little Zion of his own."

Not so thinks the awakened king of Judah and his subaltern chiefs. They make a great ado about the regeneration of the realm. They go through the land like the hot-headed reformers in the Netherlands; pulling down idols, and rebuilding desecrated altars, and putting a stop to ungodly rites of worship. Small chance is theirs if they try to keep the business secret. "They sware unto the Lord with a loud voice, and with shouting, and with trumpets, and with cornets." Camp-meetings and tent-preaching and tabernacles are a small matter compared with this uprising of a whole nation. It is more like the up-springing of our country when Sumter fell. We made no silent affair of that.

Religious men in earnest are too much in earnest to be still about it. They are moved by a great power. It will express itself as becomes a great power. Out it will come in speech, in act, in prayer, in song, in great enterprise, and in glad achievement. It is the instinct of religious faith to bear its witness to the world. It is not ashamed. Why should it skulk? God has given a great deliverance: men must proclaim it to those who need the same. The pearl is of great price: men will rejoice over it.

A certain degree of publicity, therefore, in a spiritual quickening of the Church, is inevitable. It is but natural. Other great awakenings work in the same way. We do not denounce the ardor of a political campaign as the hysteria of old women and sick folk. We do not call the rush to the gold-mines of California and the Black Hills cant. Why, then, judge by a different law the great awakenings of men to the realities of eternity? The Black Hills, with all their golden treasure, will one day burn to cinders in volcanic fire. The souls of the men now crowding there will then be still living somewhere, undying as God is. Where? That is the question the Church tries to answer in a great revival.

On one occasion Edmund Burke came upon the hustings to contest a seat in Parliament before an excited assembly. The people had come together with preparations for bonfires and illuminations, and processions marching to the sound of drum and fife. When he had just mounted the platform, the news came that his opponent, who was to have met him there that morning, had been just found dead in his bed. Both Burke and his hearers were so overwhelmed by that momentary opening of the eternal world to their dim vision that he could not speak, and they were in no mood to hear. He only lifted his voice for one solemn moment, and exclaimed, "What shadows we are, and what shadows we pursue!" Was that cant? Yet a revival of religion is no other than just that awakening to the reality of eternal things, and a permanent setting of the current of popular thought in that channel. Why not?

3. This old Jewish revival developed a third feature. *It was attended with a great influx of converts from without.* "The strangers fell to him out of Israel in abundance, when they saw that *the Lord his God was with him.*" So commonly works a pure revival upon the world. Very rare is the exception in which the heart of the world does not respond to the heart of the Church. Growth is the law of all life. A tree expands from the life of its root. Double the vitality there, and you double the fruitage. So is it with the spiritual life, of which the Church of God is the centre.

"They saw that the Lord his God was with him." This is the conviction with which a pure revival impresses men of the world. A feeling of awe often becomes general in a community in which the Holy Spirit is moving with great power. The consciousness of God fills hearts unused to such convictions.

Many years ago an eminent officer in the government of Massachusetts returned from Europe to his home in an inland town in which a powerful work of divine grace was in progress. He had not heard of it. As he passed through the streets, the look of things seemed strange to him. The countenances of those whom he met impressed him with a sense of something unusual. The church-bell was tolling at an unusual hour. "What has happened here?" was his inquiry. "Something is in the air. Things seem like the day of judgment." There was no mystery in this. It *was* like the day of judgment. God was there, deciding the eternal destiny of hundreds of souls. It proved so to that awe-struck man, for he was soon one of the rejoicing converts.

In the great awakening under President Edwards, men cried out in great assemblies under the overpowering sense of the reality of God's being. The same phenomenon occurred during the "Year of Grace" in Ireland. Under the preaching of the late Rev. Dr. Blackburn of Missouri, men were known to rush out of churches and off from camping-grounds, saying that they could not bear the terror of God's presence, which threatened to crush them.

Certain animals have a mysterious sense by which they discern the coming-on of an earthquake, or the presence of death, before the dull eyes and ears of humankind detect them. So there seems to be in man a spiritual sense which under certain conditions feels the presence of God as it cannot at other times. What are the pathological affections of the body, often witnessed in intense revivals, but the succumbing of the nervous system to spiritual impressions which flesh and blood cannot bear with equanimity? They are hints of that awful majesty of God which shook Mount Sinai, and which God himself expressed in the law, "No man shall see me and live."

4. A fourth feature of a true revival of religion is *a thorough reformation of public and private morals.* "Asa took courage, and put away the abominable idols out of all the land." To put away idolatrous worship was what we should call a reformation in morals. Idolatry was immorality concentrated in most hideous forms. No religious zeal could have been genuine in a monarch which did not sweep the land clean of them.

Thus in every so-called revival, the critical test of its genuineness is the inquiry, "How does it affect the real life of converts?" It is in perfect keeping with such an awakening that a temperance revival should accompany it. The most valuable fruit of Mr. Moody's work in Boston during the winter of 1876-77 was believed by sage observers to be the reformation of hundreds of inebriates and many abandoned women, — reformed because religiously converted. They attribute their reformation to no other cause than their new-found religion. The metropolitan police remarked a perceptible diminution of the crimes usually caused by rum. Rumsellers complained that their business was interrupted. There are localities in New York and Boston where once a man could not safely go unarmed after nightfall, but where now a woman can go safely at midnight; and the power which has wrought the change is the work of a few Christian women in mission-schools.

That dishonest men become honest; that false men become true; that drunkards become temperate; that vile men become pure; that lost women recover the purity of their childhood; that men of intrigue and sharp dealing become guileless in act and speech; that profane men become reverent; that sabbath-breakers are found in the house of God, — these are among the legitimate tokens of a great and general revival, which are to be reasonably looked for if it is a work of God. One of the most significant evidences of conversion was given by a poor and ignorant man to a committee of examination for his admission to the church when he said, "I don't know what religion has done for me in my business, except that I have burned my bushel-measure."

An apparent religious awakening which does *not* result in making converts more honest, more truthful, more pure in private morals, is not worthy of trust. God is not in it. The payment of honest debts; dealing in trade by equity rather than by law; the giving-up of tricks of trade; a living price for slop-work; the sale of pure milk; the surrender of trades which are inimical to public morals; the destruction of distilleries; the refusal to lease houses for immoral uses, and hotels for the sale of alcoholic liquors; care not to be ignorant of such leases; suffering loss of dividends for the observance of the Lord's Day; the honest report of property to assessors; a fair day's work when working for the Government; refusing to cheat the post-office; truthful invoices of imported goods; honest oaths at the custom-house; in a word, *freedom from guile* in transactions of business, — these are among the proper fruits of a revival of religion. The world has a right to look for them. The world is right in heaping its indignation and contempt on any religious epidemic which does not prove its right to exist by these plain signs of a live conscience in worldly affairs. Shall a man be a smooth and smiling communicant in God's Church, doing service, it may be, at the Lord's table, and at same time a fit candidate for the penitentiary? God is on the side of the world in its indignant protest. "Your new moons and sabbaths, and calling of assemblies, I cannot away with; incense is an abomination unto me; when ye make many prayers, I will not hear."

Of all compounds of human weakness and depravity, the most repulsive is a bonfire of religious cant, which is all feeling and no principle, all talk and no character, all prayer and no life, all Sunday and no week-day. Ye whited sepulchres! Ye generation of vipers! The holiest of men join the indignant outcry of the world against such

AN ANCIENT REVIVAL OF RELIGION. 53

nauseating hypocrisy. That is a wise and always timely petition of the Church of England: "From the *deceits* of the world, from the *crafts* of the Devil, good Lord, deliver us!"

5. One other fact suggested by this ancient model of a revival is, that *often such awakenings are followed by periods of temporal prosperity*. "The Lord gave them rest round about." In that semi-civilized age the symbol of all temporal calamities was a state of chronic war, and the symbol of all temporal blessings was a state of peace. Rest from civil and foreign discord meant the prosperity of the arts of peace. The encouragement of industry, the increase of property, the unity of families, the preservation of young life, the growth of the able-bodied population, the increase of the comforts of civilization, and the advance of the general culture, all attended long-continued peace. This was the blessing which God gave as a sequence of the quickening of the national conscience.

Not always do all forms of temporal blessing attend repentance and holy living. But such is the *tendency* of a godly life. The promises of God have never yet been tested by the spiritual conversion of an entire nation. That test the Christian religion is to receive in the golden age which prophecy promises to the Church. The cessation of war and intemperance alone would double the property of the globe in a single generation.

All that facts bear witness to at present is that the *drift* of religious living is to better a man's worldly condition. Many a country village has been improved in its physical condition — in the comfort of families; in the lessening of poverty; in the peace of neighborhoods; in the charitableness of conversation; in the obedience of children; in the fidelity of parents; in the refinement of amusements; in the adornment of streets; in the beautifying of cemeteries; in aspirations toward literature, art, and general culture — by a thorough renovation of its society through a powerful revival of religion. No other civilizing power equals that of pure religion. It never hurts a man, for any of the right uses of this world, to make a Christian of him.

CHRISTIAN ALLIANCES WITH WICKED MEN.

And Jehu the son of Hanani the seer . . . said to king Jehoshaphat, Shouldest thou help the ungodly, and love them that hate the Lord? — 2 CHRON. xix. 2.

IT is wonderful at how many points the biographies of the Old Testament touch modern life.

"Shouldest thou help the ungodly, and love them that hate the Lord?" Such is the reproof addressed by the prophet to the king of Judah. Jehoshaphat seems to have been a good sort of man, as the world goes, — better than the average of his age. "Good things are found in thee," is the kindly judgment of the prophet about him. But he was an ambitious man. He wanted to stand well with the world. He aspired to the glory of a splendid reign. To promote his political aspirations, he sought alliance with one of the most impious princes of the time, and an apostate from the true religion. As the monarch of a theocratic government he could hardly have done a worse thing.

Jehoshaphat was a representative man, — representative of a large class of good men in every age, who for selfish ends choose their friends from among the irreligious and the worldly.

1. The friendship of wicked men is *one of the most dangerous social temptations to which Christians are subjected*. Modern life in cities illustrates it with special force.

The *wealth* of the world is very largely in the hands of men who are not the friends of Christ. Wealth is a great power. It commands respect. Honestly gained and properly used, it deserves respect. It is not necessarily a sin to desire the friendship of the rich.

In many communities *intelligence and culture* also are possessed mainly by the irreligious. Religion often thrives best amongst the poor and the illiterate.

> "Not many rich or noble called,
> Not many great or wise:
> They whom God makes his kings and priests
> Are poor in human eyes."

They who heard Christ gladly were the common people. "Have any of the rulers believed on him?" His chosen apostles were humble tradesmen and fisher-folk.

Irreligious men are often very bright men. They are brilliant conversers, ready wits, racy in thought and speech. Even profane men are forcible talkers. The society of such men is often fascinating. Fun, repartees, humorous anecdote, though not forbidden by the Christian religion, it must be conceded, are not its strong points. Irreligion often seems to have a monopoly of them. The joy of a godly life does not depend largely on the risible faculties. The young, therefore, often find powerful allurement to irreligious friendships in the social brilliancy of those who are living without God.

The *interests of business* sometimes create a similar peril. Two men once took the lease of a hotel. One was a professing Christian, the other not. The enterprise threatened to bankrupt them both. Nothing could save them but the secret and illegal sale of intoxicating drinks. The Christian partner's faith was not strong enough to withstand the resolute selfishness of the other.

In a higher circle of life *professional success* often tempts a young man of aspiring mind to seek to ally himself with those who love not God, and care nothing for his cause. Many years ago a young lawyer, who afterwards became a member of the House of Representatives of the United States, was a member of an obscure church in the mountains of New England. So long as he remained nestled among the hills, he was faithful to the religion of his fathers. But his professional prospects required him to migrate to the metropolis. There he found himself in a new world. The faith of his childhood was unpopular. Very largely it was the faith of the poor and the middling classes of society. The wealth, the culture, the social rank, the professional prestige, of the community, were compacted in almost solid phalanx against it. Prejudice against it ran so high, that the churches in which it was preached were branded with opprobrious nicknames. Their worshippers were hustled in the street.

It was a severe temptation to the youthful and brilliant lawyer, who may have felt that he had the making of a great statesman in his brain. The necessities of his professional future — yes, of his professional usefulness — seemed to compel him to abandon the old faith of the Pilgrims, and to seek association with the magnates of the bar and bench by casting in his lot with those who denied Christ. He fell before the temptation. From that time to his death, his religious faith, though probably not theoretically changed, was clouded over, and practically buried under his professional alliances.

This form of trial is often not only severe, but insidious. The wiles of a crafty adversary seldom create one more plausible and alluring. There seems to be no escape from it, and often nothing fatal in it. Men find themselves confronted by a compact and insurmountable wall of circumstance, which shuts them in and hedges them around. As they see things, no course is left to them, but to choose their friends from the secret or avowed enemies to the cross of Christ. Said an excellent Christian lady not long ago, "Almost my entire circle of friends is made up of those who have no sympathy with my religion. In the city where I live, there are no others with whom I can associate on terms of social equality."

2. Of this trial of Christian principle, it should be further said, that *the Christian religion requires no narrow or ascetic seclusion from the world.* "I pray not that thou shouldest take them out of the world, but that thou shouldest keep them from the evil." Such was the *sensible* prayer of our Lord for his disciples. No fanaticism here. It is our chief discipline for a better world, to learn to live as a good man should in this world.

A crystal is sometimes formed in the embrace of a bowlder of granite. To clear it of its rough enclosure, and to bring its beautiful facets to the light, Nature submerges it in deep waters, shatters it by tempests, and abrades it by contact with stones and mud, and the rubbish of the sea. Thus a redeemed soul is by the plan of God immersed in the cares and toils and enticements and usefulness of a world of sin, so that by sheer resistance to evil, and abrasion with depravity, it may be polished to the transparent image of Him who made it.

The thing which Christian principle forbids is the seeking of worldly friendships and alliances for selfish ends, and to the peril of religious usefulness and religious character. Every Christian's good sense discerns the distinction, and acknowledges its reasonableness.

3. Yet the irreligious friendships of religious men *violate the ruling spirit of the Scriptures*. A deliberate invitation of this form of temptation is close akin to apostasy. Gloss it over as we may, — and very ingenious and winsome are the disguises by which a deceived conscience can adorn it, — gloss it over as we please, it is a policy of life which *starts wrong*. Therefore it threatens catastrophe in the end.

The Scriptures recognize but two grades of *caste* in this world, — the good and the bad; the righteous and the wicked; the friends of God and the enemies of God. In the incisive language of the New Testament, men are all either saints or sinners. In the world, not of the world; come ye out from among them; be ye separate; a royal priesthood; a peculiar people; strangers and pilgrims on earth, — such are the *mottoes* by which inspired wisdom indicates the followers of Christ. The very being of the Church is for the purpose of keeping alive and fresh in human thought that old distinction between saint and sinner. Between the two the great gulf is fixed. They drift asunder in this world, as they are to be kept asunder in the next world.

Now, a Christian who subjects his Christian faith to worldly policy in the choice of his associates in life strikes right athwart the whole range of scriptural command and admonition and expostulation and example. No Christian can safely do that.

The statesman to whom I have referred, with all his brilliant ingenuity, did not escape the apparent wrecking of his religious faith on this rock. From the hour in which he deliberately abandoned the religious connections of his youth, the spirituality of his religious character declined. He was never afterwards known to the world as even a professing Christian. Though nominally such, he mingled with men for years, and they never knew it. He was practically a man of the world, a lover of the world, an honored leader of the world, worthy of all the dignities he received, and more, but an alien from the people of God. He lost his reverence for the Christian sabbath. He forsook, for long intervals, the Lord's table. Even to the laws of Christian morality he became treacherous. His veracity, his honesty, his temperance, his chastity, all were submerged in his intense and overmastering worldliness before he died.

Though, at the last, a few not very positive words on his death-bed left his Christian friends not utterly without hope that he died a penitent believer, yet his public career of more than forty years belied the hope. For the great distinctive ends of Christian living and usefulness, his life was a failure. It ended a blackened ruin of that which had a splendid beginning, and gave magnificent promise for the future.

4. This suggests that entangling alliances with

the world *often involve an immense sacrifice of Christian usefulness.*

A man cannot be greatly useful as a Christian without great positiveness of religious character. It lies in the very nature of our religion, that a man must believe it with his whole soul. He must give his whole being to it. In a divided heart it cannot live. One who tries the experiment pulls down with one hand what he builds up with the other. He drenches every sacred fire he kindles. He does not win the world to Christ. The world wins him.

Such a man is commonly a dead weight in the Church. If not that, he owes what good influence he has to other things than his religion. A spiritual power in the Church he is not, and cannot be. He never heads a forlorn hope on God's side of things. If he is even a silent looker-on in the conflict, and not an active opponent of the more spiritual developments of Christ's kingdom, that is the best that can be hoped for from him.

Such men are very apt to be opposers of revivals. In great awakenings they are ultra conservatives. Their instinct is to carp at or ignore such movements. The enemy of souls often finds in a group of such men his most efficient auxiliary. When at last death surprises them into a more truthful view of things, they often die mourning over a wasted and perverted life.

An old English proverb says, "He must have a

long spoon who would sup with the Devil." The saddest feature in the career of such men is that Satan most disastrously outwits them. They do not build as they think to build. They are beguiled, hoodwinked, led blindfold, to the loss of all that a child of God should hold most dear. They are Samsons: mighty, it may be, in resources of worldly prowess; great against foxes, lions, bears; but weaker than an infant in the lap of Delilah, and blind captives in the prison-house of Philistines.

5. Christian alliances with the wicked *do not command the respect of the very men for whose favor they are formed.* Men of the world are very keen in their judgments of Christian character. They know what is consistent Christian living, when they see it, as well as we do. Indeed, their theoretic ideal of a Christian life is commonly more exalted than that of men who are struggling to realize it. No other class of men are so prompt to tell us what they would do if they believed as we do, as those who believe nothing. An upright and downright Christian they always revere. In heart they make obeisance to him as to no other type of man. Do you not know a godless man who professes to have lost all faith in religion, but who makes exception of some one humble Christian woman, — his mother perhaps, or sister, or wife? " If ever human being gets to heaven, she will," is his testimony. That one life keeps open to his faith the celestial gates.

Said Walter Scott, on one occasion, to his daughter, — substantially, I quote from memory, — "I know this world; I have read many books; I have known many splendidly educated men in my time; but I declare to you that I have heard more lofty and noble sentiments from the lips of poor, uneducated men and women in times of trouble, than I ever met with elsewhere outside of the pages of the Bible." Yes, the world reveres the honest principles of our religion in plain, honest lives.

By the same instinctive insight into facts, they recoil with contempt when they encounter men or women who sacrifice those principles to worldly policy or social ambitions. They never at heart trust such a man. They may use him as they do other tools; but they never love him in return, because they cannot trust him.

In religion, as in other things, few things command the respect of the world like courage. Fidelity to honest convictions, conformity of heart to the faith of the head, the struggle at least to make the heart tally with the profession, the world bows reverently to these things always. Men will bear to be browbeaten by an act of religious fidelity better than to be fawned upon. They tolerate a fanatic sooner than a traitor. We all respect a pugilist more than we do a coward. A professing Christian never makes a meaner blunder than when he thinks to flatter wicked men, and win their good-will, by trampling on his deepest convictions, or ignoring his most solemn vows.

6. Loving those that hate God *inflicts a wound of great severity on the feelings of the Lord Jesus Christ.* When a young man is choosing his life's companions, Christ is looking on. When a young woman is wavering between the Church of Christ and the world, in her choice of the dearest friend she is ever to know, Christ is watching the trembling scales.

Every professed follower of his, Christ regards as his personal friend. He loves him as if he were the only friend left him. Picture his look on the scared Peter. Think of him in Gethsemane saying, "Could ye not watch with me one hour?" See him on the cross, turning his languid eyes in search of his hiding disciples. Every *one* who bears his name, he remembered and thought of in that supreme hour.

To-day he longs for your friendship, my brother, as if there were no other one in the universe to share the gift of his life's blood. He would have died for you alone, as readily as for countless millions. Hear him: "I was hungry, and ye gave me no meat; I was thirsty, and ye gave me no drink; I was sick, and ye took me not in." Deeds of common human kindness, such as we lavish on a stranger, he longed for. He longs for them now. From you, from me, from each *one* whom he died for, he craves the human love which is so precious to us all. Love is hurt if it is not loved in return.

What, then, must his feelings be when he sees

one who *has been* his friend, turning coldly from him, and choosing in his place the friendship of the world which crucified him, and which would crucify him again? My brother, it is not so much that you are losing Christ, as that Christ is losing you. It is from Calvary that the voice comes now to each one of us in our solitude: "Shouldest thou love them that hate the Lord?"

HONORING GOD'S HOUSE.

And it came to pass after this, that Joash was minded to repair the house of the Lord. . . . And he gathered together the priests and the Levites, and said to them, Go out unto the cities of Judah, and gather of all Israel money to repair the house of your God from year to year, and see that ye hasten the matter. . . . So the workmen wrought, and the work was perfected by them, and they set the house of God in his state, and strengthened it.—2 CHRON. xxiv. 4, 5, 13.

IT is popular in our day to decry as superstition that devout instinct which reveres a Christian temple as God's peculiar dwelling-place. Cold-blooded men say, "It is no more than any other mass of bricks and mortar." Poetry, too, has much to say of worshipping God in fields and forests and mountains and valleys, and on the sea. A good deal of watery sentiment has been expended by sabbath-breakers on "Nature's first temple."

The undoubted truth of God's omnipresence is about all the truth there is underneath this popular twaddle. Let us see, then, what reason we have for regarding a place of Christian worship with peculiar reverence.

1. *The biblical history of the idea of a place where*

God is worshipped represents it as one of peculiar and awful sanctity. The development of the conception of "the Lord's house" in the Scriptures is deeply interesting. The most ancient hint of it in any known literature is found in the Book of Job. "Nature's first temple" was as magnificent then as now; yet the afflicted patriarch laments, "Oh that I knew *where* I might find Him, that I might come even to his *seat!*" He longs to fix upon some *spot* where he can find God,—some *place* where the awful distance between him and God shall be lessened. Just because God is everywhere, he seems, to himself, to find him nowhere.

This is human nature. Call it infirmity if you will: still it is human nature. The intuitions of the race have acknowledged it. Groves, mountains, grottoes, caves, streams, valleys, plains, lakes, as well as altars and temples, have been consecrated as the abodes of gods. As we instinctively clothe our conception of God in human form, and seem to hear his voice, dread his eye, see his hand, hear his footfall, so we intuitively assign to him some place which we approach with awe. Is this all falsehood? It is not like God to make the soul of man a liar in its very nature.

"Nature's first temple" was as grand and imposing in Abraham's day as now: yet he went three-days' journey with his costly sacrifice to Mount Moriah; and there, in a definite and becoming *place*, he found and worshipped God. Isaac was fond of walking in the fields at eventide; but he built an altar at Beersheba, because God there appeared to him, and blessed him. The heavens were resplendent with the constellations of a Syrian sky when Jacob spent a night in the open plain. The ground was his couch, and a stone was his pillow. But he discovered before morning that God was there; and he called the place Bethel, and said, "How dreadful is this place! This is none other than the house of God; and this is the gate of heaven." Again he spends a solitary night under the open sky, and his dreams are troubled. He seems to be struggling with an august and mysterious stranger till the daybreak. And he calls that place "Peniel;" for, says he, "I have seen God face to face."

Moses is keeping flocks near Mount Horeb, and a bush on fire turns him aside. He thinks it "a great sight," for he discovers that God is there. He hears a voice saying, "Draw not nigh hither: put off thy shoes from off thy feet, for the place whereon thou standest is holy ground." Again, when Moses leads the people out of Egypt, not every man's tent is God's dwelling, but a pillar of cloud and of fire leads the march, and God is in the pillar. Arrived at Sinai, amidst thunder and lightning and tempest and fire, and "a voice of words," God is found high up in the mountain and the cloud. Moses goes up into the thick darkness where God is. There he receives the pattern of the tabernacle, and that becomes for generations the peculiar mercy-seat of God. The people fear exceedingly, and tremble, and cry out, "Let not God speak with us, lest we die!"

At length the kingdom of Judah reaches its golden age; and the temple rises in far-famed splendor. God says of it, "I have *hallowed* this place, to put my name there forever." The temple of Solomon was the original ideal of a house of God, realized in architecture unrivalled in that age. A whole nation poured out its treasures in the building. The wisest of monarchs tasked the skill of the most ingenious artificers, and the genius of the most accomplished architects of the times. It was the Jewish St. Peter's. Ophir sent its pure gold, and Lebanon its magnificent cedars. Jerusalem and Tyre united their navies as transport ships. "The house of God" must be made "exceeding magnifical, of fame and glory throughout all countries." So hallowed was the place, and so sacred the work, that it must proceed in hushed stillness. Because God was to dwell there, "neither hammer nor axe, nor any tool of iron," must be "heard in the house while it was in building." It must grow in silence, as forests grow.

> "No workman's steel nor ponderous axes rung:
> Like some tall palm the noiseless fabric sprung."

When finished it was one of the wonders of the world. The reporters of the age could not tell the half of it. Sheba's queen was abashed as she approached it, and "there was no more spirit in her."

Such is the biblical conception of the sacredness of the house of God. "The holy place; the holy hill; the place where mine honor dwelleth; the gate of heaven:" so the Bible describes in brief its unutterable sanctity.

2. *The Bible represents the building and repairing of the Lord's house as acts of eminent piety.* The historian says of Joash in the context, that he was a godly man as long as he had the guidance of the celebrated priest Jehoiada. Yet the only thing thought worthy of mention in that part of his reign is, that "he was minded to repair the house of the Lord."

It was counted an act of signal devotion in David, that he was minded "to build the house of the Lord." Only the awful sacredness of the work forbade David's doing it, because he had been a man of war. It was incongruous with the divine idea, that a military chief, who had shed much blood, should set his hand to a work so holy. The dignity of a great civilian, and the most highly cultured monarch of the age, was better suited to its hallowed purpose. Of Solomon's long and splendid reign, the erection of the temple was the crowning deed, renowned alike as a token of his wisdom and his piety. The chief object of one entire book of the Bible — the Book of Nehemiah — is to record the building of the second temple.

Passing on to later times, the most significant token of the divine idea of the temple where God dwelt is found in the fact that our Lord accepted it as the symbol of his own sacred body. "He spake of the temple of his body." His resurrection, the crowning event of his sinless life, was a rebuilding of a temple. When the apostles also would express to Christian believers the most exalted conception of their consecrated character in God's sight, the form of the admonition is, "Ye are the temple of God. Whoso defileth the temple of God, him shall God destroy."

3. In perfect keeping with the biblical idea on this subject, *it is the instinct of a devout heart, everywhere and always, to revere the house in which God is publicly worshipped.* Like every other vital principle of religion, it may degenerate into superstition. But it is natural to the spirit of worship. Catholic Christians are right in their reverent regard for their churches and utensils of service. If Protestant Christians have lost the ancient spirit of the Church in this respect, they are none the better for it.

An incident occurred in Boston not long ago, which made me wish that all our churches were open for daily and hourly individual worship. A poor emigrant-woman, with her helpless children, apparently just from the ship in which they had come to a strange land, saw a Protestant church, on the spire of which was the familiar cross. She thought it a temple of her own faith. But, as its doors were closed, she could not enter; and she devoutly knelt with her children on the pavement, and offered silent prayer. She was a stranger in a strange land. Strange faces and sounds which she could not understand were all around her; but there was one thing which was familiar and dear to her, — the cross, emblematic of our common Redeemer. She could understand that. I seemed to hear her voice as her heart flowed out in grateful prayer for herself and children in the new life which they were beginning, or in thanksgiving for their safety from the perils of the sea. Was that superstition? I could not call it so.

I once sat in the shadow of one of the arches of the Colosseum at Rome, in the autumnal moonlight, and alone. That ruin has long since been consecrated as a place of Christian worship. A cross stands in the centre, around which a crowd of worshippers is often gathered on a Friday, listening to very earnest, and by no means unchristian, preaching. As I sat there trying to picture the scenes of the early martyrdoms which had occurred there, when Christian captives were thrown to wild beasts amidst the ferocious plaudits of a hundred thousand spectators in the galleries above, a solitary peasant came through; and bending under his burden of fagots, and unconscious that any human eye was looking on, he knelt and offered silent prayer before the cross. The cross was nothing to my Puritan iconoclasm; and the promise on the placard appended to it, of deliverance from I do not know how much time in purgatory to any one who shall imprint a kiss there, saddened me. But I could not judge by my severer faith the impulsive devotion of the poor Italian. I wanted to grasp his hand as that of a Christian brother. He was expressing in his way the same instinct of religious reverence which I felt in looking upon the spot where thousands of Christian martyrs had sealed their fate in blood. Who shall judge between us, and say that my mood was religion, and his superstition?

It may have been an extreme of this instinct which led Dr. Samuel Johnson to lift his hat reverently whenever he passed a church in the streets of London; but better that than the covered head and the laugh and the jest often seen and heard in our churches. That is a becoming, because a perfectly sensible, act of reverence, in which worshippers of the Church of England bow the head in silent prayer at the beginning of public religious service. Our plainer forms of worship would be improved by the usage.

4. *The associations of the Lord's house are an incalculable help to the culture of religious character.* We are creatures of association. We are often moved more profoundly than we think by our surroundings. The recollection of our experiences in the house of God may be among the most

precious treasures that memory hoards. The prayers we have heard there; the old hymns of the fathers, some of them redolent with the incense of a thousand years; the sermons which have moved us; the Scriptures read and expounded; certain texts which were new to us and most timely; the light of the setting sun streaming in at western windows when it seemed like the glory of God's countenance; the seat where the mother sat holding fast our childish hand, or the corner from which the father turned his loving eye upon us in mild reproof; the pews from which sainted men and women have gone to their rest, — oh, there are holy forces in such reminiscences! They are "golden vials full of odors." They come back to us in after-years, "trailing clouds of glory." They make the very walls of the house of God eloquent. The stone cries out of the wall, and the beam out of the timber answers it. The very silence of the place on a week-day is more potent than angels' voices. O thou homely "meeting-house" of my youth, God bless thee! If I forget thee, let my right hand forget her cunning; if I do not remember thee, let my tongue cleave to the roof of my mouth!

An eminent statesman of our country, whose funeral was attended by reverent thousands, once boasted flippantly that he "had not seen the inside of a church in twelve years." Well, he had sought other things, and he had his reward. But his character, through his long public career, showed the want of just those qualities which devout attendance on the services of religion would have tended to develop. He was irreverent, uncharitable, selfish, intemperate in speech, one-sided in policy, a man of few friends, whom all men feared but few could love. And, so far as men could see, — God knows how truthfully, — he died as the fool dieth. Not one word of Christian consolation relieved his last agonies. He uttered not one word which could indicate whether he believed in God or not, whether he had a soul or not, whether he thought of or cared for the world to which he was going. An educated Greek who had never heard of the New Testament might have died as calmly and as rationally. Socrates died *more* rationally. Many a savage in our Western wilds has died chanting his tribal death-song, with more evidence of fitness to meet the Great Spirit than that man over whose bier thousands went through the forms of magnificent mourning. "I had rather be a doorkeeper in the house of my God than to dwell in the tents of wickedness."

5. *A Christian church is the most significant emblem we have of heaven.* "This is the *gate* of heaven," said the astonished patriarch. He had seen angels. Heaven seemed very near to him.

There was reason in the simple faith of our fathers, which interpreted these words so literally that they longed to build their tombs underneath the churches where they and their fathers worshipped, or in the cheerful "God's acre" around them. They wanted to be close at hand when the morning dawned.

It was one of the strange omissions which attracted the wonder of St. John in the New Jerusalem, that he saw no temple there. But he adds as a reason, ample in his view, that the Lord God Almighty and the Lamb are the temple of it. Let us not lift irreverently the veil from these words; yet they must mean so much as this, — that in some mysterious way the ineffable Godhead will do for us there what the material temples of our worship do here. These are the antechamber to that awful yet precious Presence.

It is an inspiring thought also, that the most intelligible conception the Scriptures give us of the occupations of the heavenly life is that of churchly song. The service of song is the one grand hint which our embodied spirits can comprehend of what heaven is, and what we are to do there. Active as we doubtless shall be beyond all conceptions of our tired faculties here; migrating, it may be, in chariots of eager thought, to distant and invisible portions of the universe, — yet all that we do shall be done in the spirit of such ecstatic gladness, that we shall live in a *state* of holy and triumphant song. Melody shall express, more than any other one idea, our doing and our being.

For one, I cannot rid myself of the hope, too,

that we shall sometimes — perhaps on great anniversaries commemorative of earthly histories — literally sing the very psalms and hymns which are so often the "gate of heaven" to us here. It would be sadder parting with this world than we hope it will be when our time comes, if we must forget these ancient lyrics, or find our tongues dumb when we would utter them. How can we live without them? Are they not a part of our very being? Take them away, with all the experiences of which they are the symbol, and what would there be left of us to carry into heaven?

Some lines, at least, of the hymn "Rock of ages, cleft for me," and "My faith looks up to thee," and "Not all the blood of beasts," and "Nearer, my God, to thee," and "Just as I am, without one plea," — must we part with them? It would be like parting with the recognition of friends in heaven.

What disembodied life, if there is such a thing, may be, I do not know. To my earth-bound thought it is what I imagine the gorgeous pinions and sportive flights of the butterfly are to the caterpillar. But one thing I hope and pray for: Of old friends, and old scriptures, and old hymns, and old litanies, and old churches where the fathers worshipped their God and mine, Lord, keep my memory green forever!

PRESUMPTION IN THE WORSHIP OF GOD.

But when [Uzziah] was strong, his heart was lifted up to his destruction: for he transgressed against the Lord his God, and went into the temple of the Lord to burn incense upon the altar of incense. . . . And Azariah the priest went in after him, and with him fourscore priests of the Lord, that were valiant men: . . . And they withstood Uzziah the king, and said unto him, It appertaineth not to thee, Uzziah, to burn incense unto the Lord, but to the priests, the sons of Aaron, that are consecrated to burn incense. Go out of the sanctuary, for thou hast trespassed. . . . Then Uzziah was wroth, and had a censer in his hand to burn incense: and while he was wroth with the priests, the leprosy even rose up in his forehead before the priests in the house of the Lord, from beside the incense altar. . . . And Azariah the chief priest, and all the priests, looked upon him, and, behold, he was leprous in his forehead, and they thrust him out from thence; yea, himself hasted also to go out, because the Lord had smitten him. — 2 CHRON. xxvi. 16–20.

THE punishment of sin by bodily disease is commonly long in coming. It is one of the apparent after-thoughts of retribution in which God clearly expresses his accumulated anger against sin long ago committed, and perhaps forgotten.

The case of Uzziah is one of the few instances recorded in the Scriptures of instant and severe punishment of the sin of irreverence and presumption. God does not always punish sin in the same way. The sin is the same, age after age. It is marvellous how human nature repeats itself, but God's treatment of the wrong is infinitely diversified. That irreverent worshippers are not all lepers, is no proof that they are more pleasing to God now than when the Judæan king was rebuked by that loathsome disease.

Let us note some of the ways in which the guilt of presumption in the worship of God is often incurred in modern times.

1. It ought not to provoke a smile when the first is named as that of *sleeping in God's house*. We must not be severe — for God is not so — in judging of the aged and the infirm and the diseased, whose worn-out powers yield to the soporific atmosphere, and perhaps the more soporific sermon, on a hot Sunday in July. One of the most touching illustrations of God's charitable judgment of physical infirmity is our Lord's plaintive inquiry of his sleepy disciples in the garden, in which there is only a low undertone of reproof: "Could ye not watch with me one hour?" Think of falling asleep in Gethsemane! Could you or I have done it? Yet Christ was very gentle in his thought of his weary disciples; and so he is of us, if age or disease renders sleep irresistible. Certain insomniac patients have been known, who for the most part could sleep only in the house of God. Not to such is the infirmity charged as sin.

But when no such excuse exists, when sleep is welcomed by the hale worshipper as a means of whiling away an irksome hour, few things of the silent sort can be more *impertinent* to the most high God. Should we sleep anywhere else where God should make his awful presence known? Should we have slept through the earthquake at Sinai? Shall we sleep in the day of judgment? Even in our death-hour do we not hope at least to have all our faculties about us and wide awake? The case is too plain for argument. That man coolly insults God, who needlessly composes himself to slumber, when professing to be a suppliant for mercy at his feet.

2. Similar is the presumption of *neglecting to participate in divine worship when present in God's house.* Negative sins are sometimes most intensely sinful. Heedless sins are sometimes most fearfully fatal.

If you were one of a delegation to the Court of St. James, for the presentation of a petition, and were admitted to audience with the Queen, should you think it becoming to the dignity of the royal presence to neglect the business in hand, and to wander about the apartment curiously, while your chairman was presenting the petition in your name? Yet that which would be only a breach of etiquette there, is a much graver offence in the house of God. A listless and wandering mind roving like fool's eyes, in the temple of worship, is a most insolent indignity to the King of kings.

Look at it in another light. When the Rev. Dr.

Armstrong was wrecked with a large number of fellow-passengers on one of the Sound steamers, many years ago, his last act was to gather his doomed companions together in the shattered cabin, and, while the ship was thumping to pieces on the rocks, he committed their souls and his own to God in prayer. It was his last chance, and theirs, to pray this side of eternity. Men who had not prayed for years prayed then, with agony of desire. If you had been one of that group, would you have stood or sat in silent contempt of the solemnity? Yet you *may be* doing just that, — flinging insult in the face of God on the threshold of eternity, and tossing to the winds your last chance of prayer, — every time you listen to public worship in which you do not reverently join.

There is yet another aspect of it. Like all other presumptuous sins, the hearing of prayer without participating in the service has a peculiarly indurating effect on the conscience. The habit deadens all the moral sensibilities auxiliary to conscience. The sense of gratitude is dulled if thanksgiving to God falls on the ear without awakening response of heart. The susceptibility of penitence is blunted if confession of sin is offered in the hearing of an unanswering soul. The sense of honor is benumbed if one incurs the meanness of listening unmoved to an acknowledgment of God's claims upon one's love. A latent sense of moral propriety is deadened when reverent speech, look, attitudes, are expressed around one who gazes in stolid vacuity of thought and torpor of feeling. A delicate sense of moral beauty is drugged by the hearing of holy song to which the heart is apathetic. Men rarely appreciate how fearfully they debase and deform the most godlike faculties of their being, by the quickly growing habit of unresponsive listening to the services of God's house.

There is an insidious disease which slowly and secretly turns vital organs of the body to bone. It begins by ossifying little fragments of tissue here and there. No medical skill can arrest its progress. Nature is perverted from her healthy processes of assimilation and nutrition, to the creation in the system of nothing but bone. What should be life to muscle and nerve and sinew and arteries, turns to solid and lifeless bone. At length the heart is reached, and vital parts of it become bone, and its beautiful work of pulsation, by which life is sent in red streams to the very tips of the fingers, ceases, and death ensues. Such is the moral induration which the sensibilities of a soul suffer, when long appealed to by the services of religion, to which it will not give back a throb of responsive feeling. Ossification of *heart* may have a double meaning.

3. Presumption in worship may take the form of *frequenting the house of God as a place of entertainment merely*. "Thou art to them as a very lovely song of one that hath a pleasant voice, and

can play well on an instrument; for they hear thy words, and do them not." Thus the Lord said to the prophet Ezekiel; and it is a truthful record of the reception which multitudes give to faithful and eloquent preaching. Often the auditorium of God's house is turned end for end. It is not the pulpit, but the organ and the operatic quartette, which entertain the wondering listeners.

In a certain church the most costly music that money can buy is furnished to the worshippers. The same "stars" appear there on Sunday that stood the evening before on the stage of the opera or the theatre. An entrance-fee is charged at the door. People flock thither as to a place of religious entertainment. Many of them profess no other motive. The sermon, the prayer, the scriptural lesson, are but appendages to the performances of the operatic troupe. Is that worship? Can God be pleased with it? "My house shall be called a house of prayer, but ye have made it a den of thieves." Is it any more a sin to sell a dove in the temple than to sell a song? The only instance in which our Lord gave way to violence in his holy indignation was at the sight of the desecration of the sanctuary. Would he not find use for the whip of small cords if he should wander into certain churches in our day?

4. We are guilty of presumptuous sin in worship, if we endeavor *to conceal from ourselves hidden sin under cover of scrupulous devotion.* In

the time of the judges of Israel there lived a man, Micah by name, who stole eleven hundred shekels of silver. He built him an idol with a part of it, thus "consecrating it to the Lord" as he thought. He was an idolater and a thief. His conscience pricked him. So, to make every thing sure, he hired a young Levite to be his household chaplain. "Now," said he, "the Lord will do me good, seeing that I have a Levite to my priest." That was a semi-barbarous age. The trick of the thieving rascal seems transparent. We marvel that even an old half-civilized Jew could juggle himself with it. But are there no such self-cheated worshippers in our times? By more ingenious devices perhaps, and in more recondite twists of conscience, yet not a whit less impiously towards God, we may make our very fidelity to God's house, and the zeal of our worship, a cover to hidden sin which we are not willing to abandon, and therefore not willing to see.

A recent celebrated forger in New York was one of the most faithful attendants upon the worship of a Christian sanctuary. For years, while he was setting his hand to the deeds for which he now lies in the penitentiary, he was repeating every sabbath the prayers of an ancient church; singing the songs which the voices of martyrs had hallowed; giving freely of his stolen goods to the benevolences of God's people; and, as he seems to have believed, loving rather to do deeds of charity than to hoard gold. It would be just like man, if that poor man really persuaded himself that his religious devotions would somehow offset his crimes. Yes: that is man as he is by nature. Such are we all, but by the grace of God. Our very consciences become tortuous and serpentine under the wiles of sin, till we verily think we can mock God with impunity. Oh, how idiotic we become when we make Satan our ally!

5. We are guilty of presumptuous worship *when we offer to God services in which any essential truth of God's being is denied or ignored.* A celebrated preacher of "another gospel," recently deceased, has published as a part of the "truth as it is in Jesus," as he understood it, the following fragments: "I take not the Bible for my master, nor even Jesus of Nazareth. . . . He is my best historic ideal of *human* greatness; not without errors, and I presume of course not without sins. For men without sins exist in the dreams of girls. You and I never saw such a one, and we never shall." Let us think kindly of the erring one who has gone to a world where the "Lamb that was slain" sits as judge of the living and the dead. He has discovered before this time who and what the Lord Jesus Christ is. He has learned what that means, "Who is the brightness of his glory and the express image of his person." But can God ever have been pleased with worship which denied his triune being; with prayer which as-

sumed that the Lord of glory was a sinner; with songs of praise in which the claims of Him who "was with God, and was God," were ignored?

How God will deal in eternity with honest infidelity, if there be such a thing in the strictest and final analysis of the human heart, we may safely leave to him. I do not know, and do not wish to know. But it becomes us who believe with all our souls that Jesus Christ is indeed the Lord of glory, "very God of very God," and that in him we have an infinite and eternal and sinless Saviour, to beware how we offer, or seem to offer, worship which denies him his place on the throne of the universe. The place of worship where he is thus denied is no place for us. Prayer offered otherwise than in his name is not prayer to us. Whatever it may be to those who honestly offer it, to us it cannot be worship of the true God. We kindle unhallowed fire on a strange altar if we thus seek communion with the Most High. Our fellowship is with the Father *and his Son Jesus Christ.*

Even in our own usages of prayer, and in our own sanctuaries, we need to be most watchful of our moods, lest we pray as a regenerate heathen might pray, who had never heard of Christ; as Socrates and Plato, for aught we know, may have prayed; with no hearty recognition of the merits of Christ as our only ground of approach to the throne of grace. A redeemed sinner, who believes that he is redeemed, who knows that he has been bought with the precious blood of Christ, commits an act of fearful presumption if he ever lapses into what may, for distinction's sake, be called *unchristian* prayer. In what other form more insolent to the most high God can he take God's name in vain?

FIDELITY TO THE RELIGION OF A GODLY ANCESTRY.

And the Lord was with Jehoshaphat, because he walked in the ways of his father David, and sought not unto Baalim; but sought to the Lord God of his father, and walked in his commandments. . . . Therefore the Lord stablished the kingdom in his hand; . . . and he had riches and honor in abundance. — 2 CHRON. xvii. 3–5.

KING JEHOSHAPHAT was the son of a pious father. The chief fact about him which the Bible emphasizes is, that he was faithful to that father's instructions, and followed his example. "He sought to the Lord God of his father, and walked in his commandments." He was also the child of other godly ancestors, going far back to the beginning of the royal line. "God was with Jehoshaphat, because he walked in the first ways of his father David."

In the religion of the Old Testament, much is made of family descent. A favorite title, by which God declared himself to his ancient people, was, "The God of thy fathers." Moses at the Red Sea sang, "The Lord is my father's God, and I will exalt him." King Hezekiah made it his plea for the pardon of his people: "The good

Lord pardon every one that prepareth his heart to seek the Lord God of his fathers." Daniel prays, "I thank thee, O thou God of my fathers." Solomon at the dedication of the temple prays, "The Lord our God be with us as he was with our fathers." Moses, predicting the calamities which should come upon the nation in the distant future, imagines the lookers-on as asking, "What meaneth the heat of this great anger?" And he replies, "Men shall say, Because they have forsaken the covenant of the Lord God of their fathers."

Yes, in the theory of religion and its blessings in the Old Testament, the glory of the children is their fathers. One topic suggested by the present lesson is that of *fidelity to the faith and example of a pious ancestry.* Observe : —

1. *It is an unspeakable blessing to have been born in the line of a Christian parentage.* What language can express the thanksgivings of thousands of us for our Christian mothers? Do not many of us owe as much to the firmness and the prayers of Christian fathers? How many of us could have borne, without a wreck of character, the temptations of early youth, but for the hallowed restraints of a Christian home? The voice of family prayer is that of a guardian angel in a multitude of homes.

Much more than godly instruction and example is involved in the blessing. By a mysterious law of God's government, tendencies to character spring from the line of natural descent. Qualities of mind, natural sensibilities, the fineness of conscience, the very make of the soul, in which the elements of voluntary character germinate, come to us by no choice of ours. It is a great thing to have had that fountain of our moral being purified and vitalized by the grace of God.

The purest *blood* this world has ever known is that of a Christian ancestry. It outranks all other aristocracies. Descent from kings and emperors bears no comparison with it. Yes, William Cowper, thou art right: —

> "My boast is not that I deduce my birth
> From loins enthroned, the rulers of the earth;
> But higher far my proud pretensions rise, —
> The son of parents passed into the skies."

The *length* of the line of Christian inheritance is in many cases a reduplication of the blessing. Blessed above princes of the blood royal is a fellow-townsman of mine, who is the descendant, in the eighth generation, from a well-known English martyr, and the golden cord of whose godly heritage has never once in all that time been broken.

It is an impressive thought, what an accumulation of *prayer* surrounds an infant at its birth in such a line! It was a favorite habit of the Pilgrim Fathers, to pray for their posterity to the end of time. If "their angels do always behold the face of my Father which is in heaven," a convoy of angels must herald the advent of such an infant upon its earthly career. What a different thing is the *probation* of such a child from that of one who bears in his very blood the virus of a dozen generations of vice and pollution!

Probably in no other nation on the globe are there so many as in our own of such Christian families, who trace back their lineage through centuries of prayer and godly living. Says a historian of the early settlement of this country, " God sifted three kingdoms, that he might send choice spirits to people this continent." Many of us are living in *grooves* of spiritual blessing, fixed by answered prayer a thousand years before we were born. An eminent Christian of my acquaintance used to thank God daily for *concealed* blessings. Chief among such secret gifts is the shadowy hand of godly ancestors, stretched forth across the ages in benediction on our heads.

2. *The religion of our fathers, because it is such, has a strong presumptive claim upon our faith.* The presumption may be balanced by opposing evidence; but, till it is thus neutralized, it exists in the case of every man. It is no dishonor to a young man to believe in the religion of his father. It shows no want of independence to be a Christian because one's father was a Christian. To believe as my father believed, to trust the faith

which my mother sang to me, to cling to the Christian hopes which first bloomed at the fireside of my childhood's home, to rest in my *inherited* religion, and follow the example of my godly parents, is no unmanly thing. God forbid that I should glory in breaking loose from such sacred ties! Said a clergyman of my acquaintance, "I have been young, and now am old, and I have spent my life in the study of the religions of the world; but I have yet to find a stronger proof of the truth of the Christian Scriptures than I discovered forty years ago in the character and life of my father and mother."

That pride of intellect which a young man sometimes feels, which makes him think that nothing in religious faith can be *settled* by the past, that he must therefore inquire *de novo*, as if no experience had taught his ancestry any thing, is a very weak and narrow affection of the brain. No generation exists, in God's plan, for nothing. Every generation of Christian believers adds something to the reasonable faith of the world in Christ, as truly as every generation of astronomers furnishes data for the calculations of astronomers who follow them. I have no more reason for rejecting the Christian faith of my father because I have not investigated every thing about it, than I have for going back to the Ptolemaic theory of the stars because I am not an expert in the Copernican astronomy.

3. *It is one of the divine laws of the increase of the Church, that the children of Christian parents should themselves be Christians.* The conversion of this world to Christ is not to be brought about by revivals of religion alone. There are laws of grace as well as laws of nature. There is a law of Christian *nurture*, by which, through the grace of God, every Christian family becomes a nursery of the Church of Christ. Such is God's obvious design. *Character* is not transferable from father to son, but the *elements* out of which character grows are so. Religion once rooted in a Christian family should achieve so much *conservation* of Christian forces. A moral dike is thus built up against the floods of depravity, behind which children may be safe, as Holland is from the inroads of the sea.

There is no good reason why our children should not *grow up* into Christian faith, instead of being wrenched into it by moral convulsions after years of riot in depravity. Plant an acorn anywhere, and anyhow, in good soil, and it will grow upward, and not downward. By the law of its being it seeks the sun. So a child set in the groundwork of a Christian household, and nurtured in its holy light and atmosphere, should by the very conditions of his existence grow up towards God and heaven.

Many do thus grow up Christians. Many Christian men and women cannot remember the day when they did not love God and trust in Christ. A Christian childhood may be reasonably expected to be free from flagrant vices. The very birth-hour may be the hour of holy regeneration. Christian training may be the medium of sanctifying grace. By this law of religious nurture, as well as by that of great awakenings from a godless life, it is God's design that the Church shall grow, till it covers all the families of the redeemed. One such family is in God's plan the fountain of a pure stream which is to widen and deepen till it flows in holy majesty into eternity.

4. *The imitation of a godly ancestry is peculiarly pleasing to God.* It is everywhere so represented in the Scriptures. Says St. Paul to Timothy, "I thank God when I call to remembrance the unfeigned faith that is in thee, which dwelt first in thy grandmother Lois and thy mother Eunice." The transmission of godliness to the third generation is here the theme of thanksgiving.

God is pleased with honor paid to his own laws. When he has given to a young man the inestimable blessing of a Christian parentage, he looks to see the blessing recognized. It is a joy to Christ to see a youth treading in the steps of a Christian father, and praying to old age the prayers taught by a Christian mother. Such a life honors God's mode of procedure. It is the supreme form of obedience to parents, with which God is well pleased. When Christian living follows a long line of godly progenitors running back through centuries of grace, there is an accumulation of glory to the gracious plans of God which cannot but be a joy to him.

5. *It is an act of signal and relentless guilt, to break the line of a pious heritage by a godless life.* It involves a terrific contest with God for the damnation of the soul. Tough is the task which such a young man sets himself, to destroy his soul. He must do it fighting against the most potent devices of God for his salvation. Father's counsels, mother's prayers, godly example, the indefinable atmosphere, like to none other, of a Christian home, the holy momentum from a long procession of Christian forefathers, going back, it may be, into unknown history, must be persistently, in dead earnest, insolently, contended with and defied.

That is a conflict more sanguinary, and of more woful issue, than any ever fought with sword or cannon on sea or land. A tripled and quadrupled cordon of spiritual influences must be charged and broken through. Such forces are never overcome but by the aid of opposing forces from the powers of darkness. Such a one must achieve his destruction by inviting Satan into alliance. He must throw himself into the embrace of malignant auxiliaries. It is as if he cried out from within the reserved enclosure in which God has sought to protect him, "Come and help me to withstand God!" Oh! it is the saddest sight that angels ever look upon, when the child of a godly ancestry forces his way to hell over trampled prayers, and mangled forms of fathers and mothers extending back in the shadowy past perhaps a thousand years.

Of the eminent men in American history, no one has come to the close of life under a darker cloud of reprobation from God and man than Aaron Burr. He was the son of parents eminent for piety. His father was the venerable president of a Christian college. His mother was the daughter of the Rev. President Edwards, a most godly man, and herself also a woman renowned for her rare Christian culture. The family extended far back in a luminous pathway of Christian faith and prayer. What an accumulation of holy forces was concentrated upon Aaron Burr's boyhood and early manhood! They surrounded him in no hard, repellant forms, but in the genial graces and beautiful adornments of educated Christian society. The piety of his father was lighted up by a mirthful humor. No happier men ever lived than the clergy of that age. The best education of the times, too, was his. Thus directed, so far as home and inheritance and circumstance could do it, thus directed toward heaven, he entered on his active manhood.

When approaching his twentieth year, he became interested in the salvation of his soul. The Spirit of God then clearly set before him the great alternative, and pressed his decision on the side of virtue and religion. He retired for some weeks to a rural town in Connecticut, for the sake of settling once for all the question of his religious character. Nobody knows what was the history of those critical weeks, — through what conflicts he passed, how near he may have approached to the God of his fathers, nor what fatal influences turned him back. But he came home resolved, as he said, "never again to trouble himself about his soul's salvation."

To all appearance he kept that resolution to the last. The die was cast, as he meant it should be, "once for all." It is not known that he was ever again seriously disturbed by religious convictions. He entered on what promised to be a brilliant public career, without God and without hope. He passed through it a godless man. He ended it disappointed in his ambitions, and soured against all the world. He died in obscurity, abandoned by old friends for years before, unsaluted by them as they passed him in the street, with the guilt of murder on his soul, and the brand of Cain on his brow. So far as man can know, he went speechless into eternity, with a seared conscience and a hardened heart. God suffered him, as he generally does suffer such men, to die as he had lived.

His was a representative history, — representative of those who *break the line* of ancestral piety, and force their way to an irreligious life and death, in defiance of God's protective plans for their salvation. It is an appalling question — do not angels pause, and "lean on their harps" to catch the answer? — "Who are the Aaron Burrs now living in Christian families?"

THE LOST SON OF A GODLY FATHER.

The Lord brought Judah low because of Ahaz king of Israel. And in the time of his distress did he trespass yet more against the Lord. This is that king Ahaz. . . . He said, Because the gods of the kings of Syria help them, therefore will I sacrifice to them, that they may help me. But they were the ruin of him. . . . And in every several city of Judah he made high places to burn incense unto other gods, and provoked to anger the Lord God of his fathers. — 2 Chron. xxviii. 19, 22, 23, 25.

"WHEREFORE do the wicked live?" Some wicked men are among the most useful of mankind. Certain poisons medical science uses to fight certain diseases which yield to no other remedy. So certain examples of iniquity may be transformed by the grace of God into remedial forces, by the contrast they furnish to the virtues, and the wisdom they teach to observers.

King Ahaz is one of the stupendous monuments of guilt in Israelitish history. He is one of the few men in any history of whom not one good thing is recorded. His career was one uniform and unmitigated stream of iniquity from beginning to end. Not one virtue or virtuous act is thought worthy of mention in his whole life. So black and disgraceful was his reign, that when he died, the indignant and revolted conscience of the nation refused him burial in the royal sepulchre.

Let us inquire what lessons may be learned from the life of such a supreme model of depravity.

1. His career illustrates *that law of character by which the wickedness of a man is proportioned to the amount of holy influence which he has conquered.* We find a reason for his extreme depravity in the extreme facilities which he had for being a saint. He was the son of a godly father. His youth was passed under the restraints of holy example. He was one in a royal line which had been distinguished for examples of illustrious piety. He had good blood. He came from good stock. He knew that he alone, of all the monarchs of the world, held his crown and kingdom by divine right as king of God's chosen people. He knew that a splendid history lay behind him, and that a more splendid future was before him. In the line of regal descent, in which he was a connecting link, One was to appear in whom all the nations of the world were to be blessed. That ancient promise of God to Abraham spanned like a rainbow the royal family of Judah. Mysterious as its meaning was, it must have been a power of moral restraint and moral stimulus to a man called of God to sit on the throne of Judah.

Said a French monarch, when once solicited to consent to a dishonorable treaty, "The blood of Charlemagne is in my veins; and who dares to propose this thing to me?" The sense of honorable inheritance must have been a moral power of immense significance to a monarch who stood in a line of theocratic princes. And it was not frittered away and lost in the mere sense of chivalry: it was a direct and potent help to holy living before God. Such a combination of holy influence this Judæan king broke through; and *therefore* he became the man he was. The depth of his fall was proportioned to the momentum acquired in bursting the bonds which held him.

Such is the natural working of things in the experience of sin. It is a fundamental law of character. As virtue is proportioned in vigor to the temptations resisted, so depravity is proportioned to the forces of conscience and inheritance and education and example and persuasion, and the Spirit of God, which have been fought with and conquered. This must always be reckoned in forecasting a man's future in a career of sin. The best things perverted are the worst. Christian birth abused becomes a curse. Religious education trampled on becomes a fountain of moral disease. Sabbaths broken become an opportunity to vice. Natural sensibilities to religion, indurated by transgression, become a foundation for towering iniquity. Convictions of sin resisted are often transformed into beliefs of falsehood. The strivings of the Holy Spirit quenched become the basis of satanic conquest. Devils fill the place from which the Spirit of God has been ejected.

It used to be proverbial in the days of American slavery, that the most ferocious overseers were Northern men who had to override the convictions of their youth and their inherited faith in order to become slave-drivers. This was one variety of the universal law which governs the *degree* of character, good or bad. Tell me what good influence a man has defied and scorned in becoming what he is, and I will give you the gauge of his depravity. The worst of men are apostates from the best of faiths.

2. The career of this apostate prince illustrates also *the faithfulness of God in chastising wicked men for their good.* "The Lord brought Judah low because of Ahaz." From the beginning to the end of his reign, he experienced the truth that the way of transgressors is hard. In war he was whipped all around. In alliances he was cheated and checkmated. His people were made captives by thousands. Nothing went well with him. His public life was one long career of defying God, yet of God's persistent efforts to save him by chastising him.

This is repeated over and over again in the experience of wicked men. Such men often think it a great mystery that they suffer so much. They do not understand why it is that misfortune pursues them so. "Just my luck," says one, when ill success attends his business. Yet often the secret reason is that God is trying to save the man. He is contending with God in one way, and God is contending with him in another. There is no luck about it. It is God's faithfulness to the soul, at the expense of the pocket.

"It is a great mystery; I do not understand it: it is unjust," says an ungodly man whom disease lays low, perhaps just on the eve of splendid successes. The cup is dashed from his lips, just when he is best able to enjoy it. Ill health follows him perhaps till he is glad to find such rest as he can in the grave. Often it is no mystery. It is God's striving to save the man. It is God's faithfulness to his soul, at the cost of his body. Somebody's prayers are answered in his afflictions.

In one of the works of a popular author of fiction, a wicked man, engaged in a wicked business, is represented as scolding and swearing at and beating his Christian wife, because she persists — poor soul! — in praying for him. He protests that she shall stop praying, or he must stop his business. Both cannot go on together: one or the other must give way. He thinks he has tried it, and found it so. The fancy is often true to fact. Often prayer cannot be answered except by chastising a man. He must be whipped out of his sins, or he never can be a happy man. This is the secret of the misfortunes of many an ungodly man.

The sufferings of this world are not in the strict sense retributive. They are disciplinary. The world of retribution lies farther on. In love, God holds the rod over many a bad man. He strikes him here, and he strikes him there. God's flail threshes him like wheat. He surrounds him with trouble. He heaps up misfortunes. They come thick and fast. Life is one long disappointment. "Few and evil have my days been," is his lament as he looks backward: "all is vanity and vexation of spirit." Is not this the general feeling with which men reach old age without the consolations of religion? "Oh that I had never been born!" exclaimed Voltaire in his old age. But in this experience of the wicked, God is never vindictive. This is his way of striving to save men from eternal death. Sometimes he pursues it to the very last, till the grave closes over the incorrigible sinner, and he passes on to a world where the retributive decisions of eternity displace the benign discipline of time.

3. The life of this depraved prince illustrates further *the extreme which sin reaches when men fight successfully against God's chastisements.* "In the time of his distress did he trespass yet more against the Lord." This is the fearful phenomenon sometimes witnessed in the developments of sin in this world. Some men are not subdued by suffering. They refuse to bow to chastisement. The more they suffer, the more they sin. Trouble angers them against God. They indicate their growing fitness for the world of woe in this induration of heart by which susceptibility to the softening

effect of sorrow is destroyed. Sometimes this phenomenon is witnessed on a large scale. Times of pestilence are proverbially times of unusual wickedness in great cities. The plague in London developed the vices of the metropolis frightfully. Men patrolled the streets singing ribald songs beside the dead-cart. In the peril of shipwreck, two classes of sufferers are often observed, — those whom the peril subdues to prayer, and those whom it drives to the rum-bottle.

When the Pemberton Factory fell, two classes of sufferers were crushed under the ruins, and two sets of voices came forth from the smoke and flame. The favorite hymns of the Methodist Church from the one drowned the curses and imprecations from the other. Thus the two went up on those wings of fire to meet God. How like to the contrast of the two crucified thieves! "Lord, remember me;" and, "If thou be the Christ, save thyself and us."

Few things are so truthful a touchstone to the character of men as the way in which they treat the suffering which God sends as chastisement. One man turns at its bidding, and becomes an heir of glory: another defies it, and becomes a monument of perdition. Lord, who maketh us to differ?

4. The reign of this wicked monarch illustrates *the disappointments which wicked men experience in their hopes of happiness in sin.* The historian

relates of him: "He said, Because the gods of the kings of Syria help them, therefore will I sacrifice to them, that they may help me. But *they were the ruin of him.*" True to the life, every word of it! In no more truthful figure can we express the experience of many young men who enter on a career of worldliness. They see other men living for this world alone, as it seems to a looker-on, on the top of the wave of human felicity. A rich man seems to them a supremely happy man. A successful statesman appears to have all that an aspiring man can ask for. A man who has gained the summit of social rank and splendor becomes, to many who are below him, the model of earthly bliss. Any man at the top of the ladder seems very high up to a man at the bottom. So a young man is apt to look on the world to which he proposes to devote his being. "The world makes these men happy," he says; "and I will try it, that it may make me happy too." This is the secret experience, probably, of all who give themselves deliberately to a life of irreligion. They are allured by the glamour of irreligious prosperity.

But, when they try the experiment for themselves, "it is the ruin of them." The fruit turns to ashes. No such young man ever finds the world to be what it looked to be when he surveyed it from afar. It is a beautiful mirage. The testimony of experience is proverbial, that the richest men are not the happiest men. The most successful ambitious men are not the happiest men. The pleasure-seekers who seem to have their fill of all they planned for in life are not the happiest men. One word expresses the issue of all such experiments, — disappointment. This world is full of soured and disappointed men. The more irreligious men are, the more profoundly they experience this inward consciousness of *failure* in their life's plans. They have "hewed out to themselves broken cisterns that can hold no water."

In one of Hawthorne's thrillingly fearful fictions, he represents a wretched man going about with a serpent in his bosom. Every now and then he clutches at his breast with his fingers, crying, "It gnaws me; it gnaws me!" As he walks the streets among his kind, he thinks he finds that every man he meets is cursed with the same snaky guest in his bosom. Each man at intervals seems to thrust his hand up to throttle the reptile. All alike are doomed to the hideous companionship. "It gnaws me; it gnaws me!" is the universal confession. The whole world seems to his crazed fancy to be at the mercy of vipers, each man warming and cherishing his own.

Such a world is *any* world of beings given over to seeking happiness in itself. Such is this world, except as its fearful consciousness is relieved by the grace of God. Such is *self* in any man or woman, when turned away from God and turned *inward*. No flagrant crimes like those of the

Judæan king are necessary to reduce a man to this condition of inward and conscious *curse*. Perjury, arson, murder, are not the only nor the most common precursors of such a doom. A man has only to abandon God, and live to himself, and he is as sure of it as Judas. Such a man may sit on the throne of the Cæsars, or revel in the wealth of "farthest Ind;" yet he carries the snake in his bosom. In his honest hours, when he confesses the truth to his own soul, his ghastly soliloquy is, "It gnaws me; it gnaws me!"

5. The career of this wretched prince illustrates *the distinction which it is possible for a man to gain in this world as a monument of guilt.* "He did trespass more against the Lord. *This is that king Ahaz!*" Such is the reflection of the annalist, after enumerating the monarch's crimes. "This is that king Ahaz. Look at him; mark him! let him stand in history as a monster of iniquity; let the world stand aghast at him." Such seems to be the spirit of the inspired recorder. We all naturally crave distinction, — one man for one thing, another for another: all hanker for it in something. Any thing to lift us up and out of the common herd! This is the temper of a world without God. It is possible for a man of reckless impiety to become illustrious for guilt, and that only. Some such names stand out in history, and will stand thus forever. Where all are sinners, some become guilty above their fellows, — princes in depravity;

royal dukes in iniquity; men so like to Satan in character, that he dwells with and takes possession of them before the time.

This, I repeat, is possible to any man. It requires no great genius or invention. A man need not travel far and explore distant seas to gain the means of this hideous renown. It requires only a strong, persistent, and selfish *will*, determined to fight God. This is the natural drift of sin. What a scaffold is among human punishments, what hydrophobia is among deadly diseases, such may a man become among his fellow-sinners, by simply giving himself *to* himself, and defying the rights of God.

This is the legitimate ending of a long career of alternate chastisement and sin without repentance. A Cornish proverb says, "He that will not be ruled by the rudder must be ruled by the rock." This is the rock on which haughty and defiant guilt is wrecked. It is simply *left to itself*, to become what it has chosen to be,— such a demon of iniquity as to be abhorred of God and man. God save us from ourselves! We carry within us the elements of hell, if we but choose to make them such. Ahaz, Judas, Nero, Borgia, Alva,— all were once prattling infants in happy mothers' arms. The first babe of our race — a marvel of joy to the first mother — was the first murderer. Who shall dare to encounter the possibilities of human guilt, without the grace of God?

THE GODLY SON OF AN UNGODLY FATHER.

Hezekiah . . . did that which was right in the sight of the Lord, according to all that David his father had done. Thus did Hezekiah . . . and wrought that which was good and right and truth before the Lord his God. And in every work that he began in the service of the house of God, and in the law, and in the commandments, to seek his God, he did it with all his heart, and prospered." — 2 CHRON. xxix. 1, 2, xxxi. 20, 21.

ONE human life illustrates the whole government of God. We live under such overshadowings of God's purposes, that at every turn we come upon something which shows forth principles which are eternal. Truth is indeed stranger than fiction. Romance cannot equal the grandeur which every human life, if read aright, discloses. Hence it is that the Bible is made up so largely of fragments of biography.

1. Studying the life and reign of Hezekiah, we discover, among other things, that *he is an illustration of the sovereignty of God in conversion.* He was one of the model princes of Judah. Yet early in his life his conversion was one of the most improbable of events. He was the son of one of the most impious monarchs that ever sat on the throne of Israel. Bad blood was in his veins. His youth

was cursed by a most polluted parental example. The abominations of Oriental idolatry were the atmosphere of his childhood. Not in the retirement of a private home, surrounded by better homes, did he live, but among the splendid corruptions of a court which set the current of popular opinion, and defiled the whole kingdom. No other spot on earth is so fatal to youthful innocence as a corrupt court. Yet there this heir to the throne was born and bred. Parental and royal example combined to make him a bad man and a worse king.

It is the mysterious lot of many other men, to be born and educated under circumstances which render their conversion to God intrinsically improbable. They seem born to vice. They are trained to immorality. Childish and even infantile lips are taught to profane God's name. This is not always the lot of the poor and the ignorant only. It was the favorite pastime of one of the statesmen of the first period of our Republic, to teach his beautiful little motherless daughter at four years of age to prattle the oaths with which his own conversation was polluted. It is one of the unsolved mysteries of God's government, that such enormities are permitted. Humming-birds seem to have a more blessed existence than the children of such impious fathers and mothers.

Yet God often enters such homes with his saving grace. He speaks the word, "Thou art mine,"

THE GODLY SON OF AN UNGODLY FATHER.

and a child of immortality is saved. Christ is swift to take such a little one in his arms, and bless it; and it becomes an heir of glory. It is like God to do sovereign things. Therefore it is like God to do things which to human view seem to border on the impossible.

2. *The conversion of Hezekiah, therefore, should give encouragement to the children of unchristian parents.* So much is often said, and justly, of the covenant of God with Christian parents, that sometimes in the contrast a cloud seems to rest over the destiny of those who do not share that blessing. Said one child of vice, "My father was a drunkard, and my grandfather was a drunkard before him; I shall be a drunkard too; we belong to a race of drunkards. I may as well accept my lot first as last: it is my fate." Said another, a man of high culture, but notorious for his ungoverned passions, "My father was just so: his boys are all so. We can't live in peace together: we never did. We are all possessed of the devil: I can't help it."

Not so does God reason. "*All* souls are mine," he declares. "The son shall *not* bear the iniquity of the father," is his law. "If he beget a son that seeth all his father's sins, and doeth *not* such like, he shall *not* die for the iniquity of his father: he shall surely live. The soul that sinneth, *it* shall die." The principle of individual responsibility is most sacredly built into the foundations of God's government. He never swerves from it the breadth of a hair. In this respect, every man, woman, and child on the globe stands alone before God, as if no other man, woman, child, had stood before them. Each one of us stands alone, — alone here, alone at the judgment, alone forever. Each sins alone, is judged alone, is saved or lost alone. The solitude in which every man dies is an emblem of the individuality of his being forever.

It is also the *way* of God to save men when to human view their salvation is incredible. He delights in miracles of grace. The early disciples could not believe that Saul of Tarsus was converted. It is not recorded that they had ever prayed for his conversion. That was the quickest way of putting an end to his persecution of them; but it does not appear that they ever thought of it. But God was beforehand with them. Saul, before they knew it, was praying for them. God loves such paradoxes of grace. Unwritten biography is full of them.

True, it is a great blessing to have been born in the line of a godly ancestry. But it is a greater blessing to have been born at all, under the grace of God, in a Christian land, amidst sabbaths, Bibles, churches, and under the gracious providences of God. Some of the best of men have been illustrations of divine grace to the worst. What of heathen converts to Christianity? Heaven is already becoming populous with the children of idolaters, liars, drunkards, thieves, adulterers, murderers. Go back far enough in the ancestral line of any of us, and we come to a generation of cannibals. What but the love of God *first* took off that ancestral curse?

3. The upright character of Hezekiah illustrates also *that the conversion of men is often assisted by their natural recoil from extreme wickedness.* The young monarch must have come to the throne in a state of disgust with his father's crimes. He must have felt the dishonor of them to the royal name. He must have seen the wretched condition of the kingdom on account of them. His subsequent life shows that as a young man he must have been thoughtful and of tender conscience. He was just the man to blush for his father's disgrace, and to recoil with a young man's pride from his country's shame. This class of influences, under the grace of God, may have been the means of his salvation. It is noticeable that his reform was begun instantly on his accession to the kingdom. He lost no time. He was evidently prepared for his work by previous thought and resolution.

This is one of the benevolent devices of God for the defeat of sin. Sin is often so used as to defeat itself. One of the reasons why it is permitted to run its course, and come to a head, is that men may see it in its hideous maturity. Only thus can we know it as it is. The delay of God in its punishment may be often due to this law. And it often works to the salvation of souls.

Even irreligious men are shocked by wickedness which exceeds their own. A young man's first knowledge of the world, when he goes out from the innocence of his childhood's home, often produces a recoil from the world's depravity. He did not know before that sin was so vile a thing. He starts back from it, and begins to feel his need of prayer. Not long ago a young man who had just entered college wrote home to his father, saying, "I did not know how wicked young men could be till I came here. I shall not get through without a wreck unless I commit myself as a follower of Christ." From that time he consecrated his life to God. God used the very enormities of sin to save him from sin.

So the child of vicious parents is often saved from vice by his early knowledge of vice. Many a drunkard's child has never tasted a drop of intoxicating drink. The Holy Spirit is ingenious in devising ways of alluring men to heaven. He draws men in backward in their recoil from hell. He uses sin to defeat sin. When a prairie is on fire, and the traveller is in danger of being surrounded and suffocated by the roaring flame, he has a way of fighting fire with fire. So the Spirit of God sets guilt against guilt. Temptation is checkmated by the very ghastliness of the crime which it proposes.

The young should cherish, then, as for dear life, their first revolt of conscience from abounding sin.

THE GODLY SON OF AN UNGODLY FATHER.

The sensitiveness of a soul not yet inured to vice is the guard which God has given for its protection. The backward spring from mature depravity is a token of moral health: it may be the prelude to the soul's conversion.

Charles IX. of France, in his youth, had humane and tender sensibilities. The fiend who tempted him was the mother who had nursed him. When she first proposed to him the massacre of the Huguenots, he shrunk from it with horror: "No, no, madam! they are my loving subjects." *Then* was the critical hour of his life. Had he cherished that natural sensitiveness to bloodshed, St. Bartholomew's Eve would never have disgraced the history of his kingdom, and he himself would have escaped the fearful remorse which crazed him on his deathbed. To his physician he said in his last hours, "Asleep or awake, I see the mangled forms of the Huguenots passing before me. They drip with blood. They make hideous faces at me. They point to their open wounds, and mock me. Oh that I had spared at least the little infants at the breast!" Then he broke out in agonizing cries and screams. Bloody sweat oozed from the pores of his skin. He was one of the very few cases in history which confirm the possibility of the phenomenon which attended our Lord's anguish in Gethsemane. That was the fruit of resisting, years before, the recoil of his youthful conscience from the extreme of guilt.

Our English word "remorse" comes from a Latin word which means "to bite back." Tender sensibilities trampled on in our youth grow rabid, like canine madness, and "bite back" upon the offender with a malignant venom which has no remedy.

4. The narrative before us illustrates the fact *that when God converts men from amidst surroundings of great depravity, he often has some great and signal service for them to do for him.* Such was the case with King Hezekiah. God summoned him to the reformation of a kingdom. He trained him for it by permitting him to see the guilt and the ruin of his father's reign. When the critical time came, he lifted him out of the slough of iniquity, and made him one of the signal examples of a godly prince, whose name should give lustre to the Jewish throne forever after.

Thus God often works in humbler life. One of the most successful clergymen in the history of the New-England pulpit was the son of a drunkard and a thief. His youth was spent in extreme poverty and disgrace. The family name was a byword. When he resolved to work his way to college and to the pulpit, his father overwhelmed him with parental curses. In that man's boyhood, his ruin for this world and the next seemed to human view well-nigh certain. "Like father, like son," said his neighbors. But God had other plans for the unfortunate youth. That masterly pulpit was preparing for him, and he preparing for it. The earthly father's curses and the heavenly Father's blessing were pitted against each other. God brought him safely through those fires of Moloch. He called him to stand in a place more honorable than the courts of kings. He became greatly successful in revivals of religion. Before his death, more than twelve hundred persons were known to him who attributed their conversion to his ministry.

God knows where to find his chosen ones. He sees them from afar. They may be born in dens of vice, and nurtured in almshouses and attics and cellars. But He who was born in a manger has his eye upon them; and he brings their feet out into a large place. They stand at last before kings. Their usefulness in the end is proportioned to the lowliness and the peril of their beginning. A popular writer of our own day says that it takes three generations to create a gentleman. It takes not half of one to create a king who shall reign with Christ a thousand years.

5. The work of King Hezekiah illustrates *the moral power of one man in effecting a great work to which God has called him*. From the narrative in the lesson it appears that the reformation of the kingdom was at first the idea of Hezekiah alone. "It is in my heart," he says, "to make a covenant with the Lord." Nobody seems to have put him up to it. No prophet came to warn or to stimulate

him. The movement grew up silently in his own heart. God and he planned it alone. Probably he had been brooding over it and praying over it for years. Men do not spring into such honor at a bound. At last he was the soul of the reform. The idea was his; the measures were his; the execution was his.

So it often is in other great works of God. Some one man heads it; puts his soul into it; gives his life to it; rouses other men, and energizes them in it. There is almost no limit to the power of a live man called of God to a great life's work. Other men fall back to the right and to the left, and let such a man go up the highway of the King, while they fall in at the rear, and acknowledge his lead.

In almost every group of Christian workers, some one such man is the confessed leader; not the man that seeks leadership, but the man whom leadership seeks. Not great men and kings alone are thus exalted. God calls them from lowly places rather. Not many noble are called. The lives of such men as William Carey and Harlan Page are immortal witnesses to what one man can do, if he is roused by great ideas, filled with a great faith, endowed with a great soul, inspired by a great hope, and sets himself to work at God's bidding and in God's way. The secret leading of such men by the teachings of the Holy Spirit is akin to inspiration. They never lie in their proposals, and never fail in their achievements.

6. The work of King Hezekiah illustrates also the *suddenness with which God often achieves by the hand of such men great changes in the progress of his kingdom.* Following the story of this ancient reformation, we learn at the end of the narrative that "Hezekiah rejoiced, and all the people, that God had prepared the people, *for the thing was done suddenly.*" It was an instance of a very rapid work of grace. Although the king had originated the movement, and set others to work out the idea over which he had long brooded, he found things ready to his hand. God had "prepared the people for it." They had been reading God's providence, as well as he. Secret currents of feeling were swelling in their hearts. All that they needed was a leader. When, therefore, the leader appeared in the person of their youthful prince, events moved quickly. Results ripened fast. Before they had time to dally over it, the thing was done. The kingdom was righted, and brought once more into line in the service of the living God.

This is another of the common laws of God's working. He prepares different agencies in different channels secretly. Each is quietly fitted to another by unseen strategy. The leader is fashioned for the people, and the people trained for the leader. Unknown to each other, men are set to thinking of the same thing. The same fire is kindled in many hearts; the same resolves are created, the same hopes cherished. Perhaps no man knows the heart of his neighbor in the thing. Each man may think he is alone in it. But by and by the time comes when things are ripe for a disclosure of God's plans. The leader appears, and unexpectedly finds that he has a large following. The people rise, and suddenly find that they have a born leader. Organization is easy. Everybody seems to have a mind for the work. The result is a great and sudden *growth* of Christ's kingdom. Revivals of religion have illustrated this law over and over again. The history of Christian missions is full of it. The abolition of American slavery illustrated it. How we used to talk and pray on that subject twenty years ago! We thought it one of the far-distant events in our coming history. Centuries hence, in some golden age, we dreamed that some happy generation of our successors would arise, who would devise some way of putting an end to the atrocious system. Nobody conceived it possible that the end was so near, and would come so suddenly. But God was fitting events to events, and men to men. Had our spiritual senses been more alert, we should have heard the chariot-wheels and the tramping of steeds. At last, when he was ready, the end came in the twinkling of an eye. Such phenomena suggest the possibility that the conversion of the world may be nearer than we think.

Who knows? It would not be stranger than some things which God *has* done, if men now living should see this world consecrated to Jesus Christ.

THE PRODIGAL SON OF GODLY PARENTS.

And when he was in affliction, he besought the Lord his God, and humbled himself greatly before the God of his fathers, and prayed unto him; and he was entreated of him, and heard his supplication, and brought him again to Jerusalem into his kingdom. Then Manasseh knew that the Lord he was God. — 2 CHRON. xxxiii. 12, 13.

FEW principles of the divine government are more vital to religion than those which govern the *transmission* of tendencies to good and to evil in the line of family descent. In previous studies we have seen some varieties of them. We have observed a son faithful to the example of a godly father, in the case of Jehoshaphat; a son defying that example to the death, in the case of Ahaz; and the son of a most impious father recoiling to the service of God, in the person of Hezekiah.

The life of King Manasseh illustrates another phase of the working of those principles. The remarkable distinction of his career is, that he is the only case clearly recorded in the Scriptures, of a youth breaking away from the restraints and example of a religious parentage, who was recovered by the grace of God, and brought to repentance.

His life is the old story, — sin, chastisement, repentance, and forgiveness. "He did evil in the sight of the Lord; he made Judah to do worse than the heathen;" "Wherefore the Lord brought upon him the host of Assyria, which bound him in fetters, and carried him to Babylon;" "And when he was in affliction, he humbled himself greatly before the God of his fathers;" "And he was entreated of him, and heard his supplication;" "Then Manasseh knew that the Lord he was God." Guilt, suffering, penitence, pardon. The story of Judah's prince is the story of to-day. Twenty-five hundred years have not changed its tenor, nor relaxed the principles of God's government which it illustrates.

1. It deserves to be noticed, that the *fall of Manasseh was an exception to the general law respecting the history of children of a godly parentage.* The charge has been exultingly used against the credit of religion, that the sons of Christian fathers are *generally* worse than others. The sons of bishops and clergymen and deacons and elders are often said to be proverbially wicked. The restraints of a religious home are sometimes criticised as tending by re-action to the extremes of vice. This assertion is not true historically. Statistics disprove it.

In a certain New-England town of some thousands of people, the records of the Christian families were once examined thoroughly to test this question. I am unable to recall the exact numbers; but the proportion of the children of such families who became religious men and women, as related to those who did not, was more than five to one. Three or four such investigations have come within my knowledge, all ending in a similar result. In the Theological Seminary at Andover, some years ago, it was found, on inquiry, that out of its hundred and twenty students preparing for the ministry of the gospel, more than the hundred were from Christian homes, and more than twelve were sons of Christian ministers. A similar inquiry, with similar results, was once instituted in Amherst College. Had the common proverb on the subject been true, no such proportions as these would have been at all probable. The reverse should be the law: the Church should look for her clergy to families in which children have not the misfortune of religious restraints to lay the foundation for profane re-actions.

The design of God in the constitution of the Christian family is to make it the fountain of all virtues, the very citadel of religion, and the nursery of the Church. The Church itself is but the family on an extended scale. In the long-run, and as a general rule, it works as God intended that it should work. The covenant of God with faithful parents is not dishonored. The Church owes to it a very large portion of her membership, and many of the most brilliant ornaments of her pulpits. It is a fact which children in Christian households should ponder seriously, that, if they do break loose from the restraints of their religious training, they become *exceptional cases* of sin against exceptional privilege.

2. This is confirmed by the fact, which the early manhood of Manasseh also illustrates, *that, when the children of the good become vicious, they do become worse than the average of wicked men.* The brief records of Manasseh's reign clearly hint this. He fell back to the disgraceful level of his grandfather Ahaz. The catalogue of his crimes is fearful. "He made Judah to do worse than the heathen," says the historian. He practised sorcery and necromancy, and restored the furnace to Tophet. He worshipped the stars. He sacrificed his own children to pagan deities. He named his son Amon after an Egyptian idol. He was the first persecutor in Judah of the true religion. He removed the ark out of the holy of holies. Tradition says that the name of Jehovah was erased from all public documents and inscriptions. His reign was a "reign of terror" to the prophets of the Most High. The secular historian says that "day by day a fresh batch of the prophetic order were ordered to execution. From end to end of Jerusalem were to be seen traces of their blood." Tradition says that the prophet Isaiah, nearly ninety years of age, perished by Manasseh's order. Yet the same tradition declares that his mother

was Isaiah's daughter. He was one of the three kings who in Jewish story had no part in the life to come, — Jeroboam, Ahab, Manasseh. His name became in Jewish annals the synonyme of infamy.

This is an obviously natural working of things. A steel spring will recoil one way with a force proportioned to the power with which it has been bent the other way. A cannon-ball dropped from the summit of a shot-tower reduplicates its velocity as it descends, and it strikes the earth with a concussion proportioned to the height of the tower. Similar is the law of character. Both virtue and depravity are in exact ratio to the resistance overcome.

The child of godly parentage therefore, if he becomes an outcast, does fall lower than the average of outcasts. In the natural course of things he becomes a more hardened sinner in the sight of God. His conscience suffers a more fatal violence. His subsequent conversion is less probable. Such is the law of natural progress in the evolution of character. This doubtless is the foundation of the proverb that the sons of ministers and elders and deacons generally become monuments of superlative vice. When they do so, they attract the attention of observers by the very extreme of their wickedness and its contrast to the homes of their childhood. The child of godly progenitors cannot tamper with temptation without incurring greater peril of the loss of the soul than that incurred by other men. Exalted to heaven in privilege, — thrust down to hell in guilt: such is the contrast as the Bible paints it.

3. The fall of Manasseh illustrates a mysterious but undoubted fact respecting the law of hereditary descent as affecting character. It is *that the virus of an evil parentage, when arrested in one generation, may pass over, and re-appear in the generation following.* This youthful prince was the son of Hezekiah, one of the best of Judæan monarchs, but the grandson of Ahaz, one of the worst.

Physicians tell us that there are certain hereditary diseases of which the inheritance is often intermittent. One generation may escape their fatal fangs, but they may appear in all their virulence in the generation next succeeding. Similar is the mystery of spiritual inheritance. The unwritten history of families discloses the fact that sometimes the Christian son of an ungodly father had a most devout grandmother, whose prayers seem to be answered in his conversion. Her godly virtues seem to hold over, and re-appear in the persons of her grandchildren.

By the same law, a vicious son of a Christian father will sometimes be found to have sprung from a more vicious grandfather. The evil blood descends, like a subterranean rivulet, through the person of his own son, and comes to the surface again in the evil tendencies of the grandson. I would not probe irreverently nor to fanciful results the mysteries of God's procedures. But these are *facts* sometimes seen in the character of the linked generations. God has deemed the principle they involve of sufficient importance to be affirmed imperatively in the third commandment of the Decalogue. King Manasseh's fall, therefore, is to the point. Evil is tenacious of life. It intertwines itself around the roots of character. Tendencies to it, once created, run in the blood. We all suffer the curse of it from the fall of Adam. Not to the destruction or the lessening of individual responsibility — no, not by a hairbreadth. But it affects visibly the conditions of probation.

The old English preachers used to make much of this law of the divine government. Moral inheritance was to them a most stupendous and practical fact. Jeremy Taylor has somewhere recorded a prayer that God will purify the inherited fountain of evil in the soul, and turn back the current from rolling downward from the father to the son. To a thoughtful man, not unobservant of the ways of God, this is a most appropriate theme of secret prayer. If I am conscious of corrupt tendencies which have been a temptation to me all my life, and which I know to have been felt and lamented, or perhaps not lamented, in the lives of my progenitors, why should I not pray, with the fervor of a father's solicitude for the salvation of his offspring, that the accursed current may stop with me? that by the grace of God it may not pass on, and deluge with temptation the lives and souls of my children?

There are rivers which come down from the summit of Oriental mountains swollen with freshets, and destructive to the tillage and pasturage of the valleys; but, as they approach the sea, they are absorbed and lost in the sands of the desert. So may we pray that inherited proclivities to sin, to vice it may be, may be arrested in their cursed flow, and be lost forever from the line of the family in which we form a link, and are appointed to work out other destinies than our own. Every Christian parent may well pray, "Lord, visit not my sins and the sins of my fathers upon the children of the third and the fourth generations!"

4. The fall of this young monarch illustrates *the power of high station and worldly prosperity to counteract the influence of a religious education.* Manasseh had all that youthful ambition could desire, to make him in love with the world. His childhood was spent in anticipation of the most splendid position in the kingdom. He was heir to wealth and dignity and the alliances of kings. Courtiers flattered him. Young men felt themselves honored by his friendship. Old men did him reverence as their future sovereign. The temptation overwhelmed him, and he fell before it.

When the sons of godly parents go astray, it is found, more frequently than otherwise, that they fall before the enticements created by their fathers' wealth, and the ease and luxury with which wealth surrounds them. I ask the principal of a large academy, what is the chief cause of the ruin of boys from religious homes; and he answers without a moment's hesitation, "Too much money." I ask the president of one of the largest colleges in New England, what is the surest protection to young men against the perils of college life; and he responds, "Poverty."

We know not what we ask when we pray for riches and worldly eminence for our children. Such prayers, answered as we wish, might just nullify our care for their religious culture, and make them the sorrow of our old age. Many a Christian father goes down to the grave, gray before his time, mourning over the vices of children whose fall is due to the riches he has hoarded for them, and the social companionship to which it has been the ambition of his life to lift them. Many of us have yet to learn to live for our children on principles which recognize our own faith in the littleness of time and the magnitude of eternity.

5. The misfortunes which followed the apostasy of Manasseh illustrate *the faithfulness of God to his covenant with godly parents*. It is noticeable that the chastisements inflicted upon the young

king were very severe. A tremendous downfall is that which precipitates a king from his throne to the dungeon of a foreign enemy. Few of the princes of Judah suffered that. But this one had been exceptionally wicked: it must needs be, therefore, that he be exceptionally chastised.

We are told, too, that in his captivity "he humbled himself *greatly*." A certain *proportion* runs through his history. A great sinner, a great sufferer, a great penitent. God works thoroughly. He is faithful in adjusting the discipline to the exigency. Whom he loves, he chastens proportionately to his necessities. He spares not the rod at the expense of the child's soul. He plans for eternity, not for time. So would we have it — would we not? — in the experience of our children.

Often is this experience repeated in common life, whether our weak souls would so have it or not. God is faithful beyond our desires. Like other wise fathers, he adjusts his dealings to the *future* judgment and desires of his children. He trusts to eternity for his justification in our sight. The prayers of the Christian father and mother for the wayward son are answered in waves and billows of affliction often, till the prodigal comes back, and humbles himself *greatly*, and says, "I have sinned against my father and my father's God."

If a star in our evening sky should stray from its orbit, it could not go beyond the reach of those laws of matter and motion which have governed it from its birth. Gravitation would still hold it, as in grooves of iron which the ages could not wear away. Such a wandering star is a wayward and ungodly son of godly parents. An outcast though he be, the subject of scalding tears and despairing prayers, yet from those prayers he can never get loose. For years and years they will hold him within the circuit of salvation. They will follow him beyond the seas. Into the most loathsome dens of vice they will pursue and surround him as with a wall of fire. To the demons of temptation they are a voice of defiance and of challenge, saying, "Ye shall not have this child of mine: so help me God!"

And often God is in the voice. I have heard a Christian mother of an outcast son say, "I *know* that my boy will yet be converted to Jesus Christ. It has been told to me in my hours of agonizing prayer. I have given him to God. He is no longer mine. I may not live to see it; but God will take care of the treasure I have committed to his keeping. I shall see my son in heaven." Who shall dare to say nay to such a trusting woman? It is just like God to do such sovereign things.

6. The salvation of this penitent prince *should be both an encouragement and a warning to those sons of Christian parents who have lost the paths of virtue.* Often is it said of the penitent thief on the cross, that *one* such case is recorded in the Scriptures,

that none may despair of repentance on a death-bed; and *but* one, that none may presume.

Similar is the twofold lesson to be learned from the recovery of this fallen monarch. He tried the fearful experiment of abandoning the God of his fathers, and becoming a monument of illustrious guilt. Through bitter disappointment and humiliating sorrow, he was saved. The Scriptures expressly contradict the Jewish tradition. But he was one of a thousand. No other such is clearly declared in the Scriptures to have run that risk with safety at the last. God *can* save a soul in such an extremity of sin; but it is like lifting to its place again a fallen star. Fallen stars generally go out in darkness.

That is an exceptional hazard which a young man incurs in such an experience. It is like crossing Niagara over the rapids, on a tight-rope. *One* Blondin out of forty millions may have done it, and reached the hither shore in safety; but would you or I risk it for that? The *general* law of God's dealings with men is that strange and unnatural wickedness shall be left to itself to work out its own penalties. This it did in the case of King Ahaz.

Place these two royal sinners side by side. Both had the example and teachings and prayers of godly parents. Both broke loose from these restraints, and ran a career of wild and defiant crime. One was saved, the other lost; one taken, the other left. Why the difference we know not. It is the way of God to do autocratic things. But woe to him who presumes upon God's regal mercy, to defy his laws and trample on his grace! The probabilities are incalculably great that he will be left to his own chosen way, and to mourn at last, —

"The thorns which I have reaped are of the tree I planted."

THE TWIN SERPENTS.

And Cain talked with Abel his brother: and it came to pass, when they were in the field, that Cain rose up against Abel his brother, and slew him. And the Lord said unto Cain, Where is Abel thy brother? And he said, I know not: am I my brother's keeper? And he said, What hast thou done? The voice of thy brother's blood crieth unto me from the ground. And now thou art cursed from the earth, which hath opened her mouth to receive thy brother's blood from thy hand. A fugitive and a vagabond shalt thou be in the earth. And Cain said unto the Lord, My punishment is greater than I can bear. — GEN. iv. 8–13.

THE story of Cain is the story of all ages. Sin, suffering; the one following the other by a law fixed and imperative like that by which pain agonizes a burning hand. A living poet speaks of

"The coils
Of those *twin serpents*, — Sin and Suffering."

So far as the narrative informs us, the suffering of the first murderer was mental suffering. Disease did not blast him; chains did not bind him; the mysterious mark on his forehead was not a burning brand. He went his way like other men. He had sons and daughters: he built the first city known in history. Tradition says that he founded many cities, and became the head of a great empire. Yet Cain "*went out from the presence of the Lord.*" He lived a life of conscious curse. The serpents coiled within. Cursed in thought, cursed in feeling, cursed in fears, cursed in blasted hopes, cursed in one long despair: such was life to the first man who bore the fruit of the first matured and ripened sin. And such will be the life of the last man who shall go out from the presence of the Lord, bearing the burden of a finished crime unrepented of and unforgiven.

Sin finds in the very constitution of the human mind the enginery of its own retribution. Let us note some of these retributive experiences of sin, as developed in the common life of men.

1. *The very consciousness of sin is destructive of a sinner's peace.* The consciousness of sin is itself suffering. "Sin revived, and I died," is the testimony of St. Paul. And this is the testimony of every sinner of every age. The bare conviction of guilt in having transgressed the law of God is the basis of the keenest anguish a man ever suffers in this world or any other.

We are so made that it cannot be otherwise. God has so constituted our nature that no man ever yet lived who felt absolutely no emotion when the naked fact of sin was laid on his conscience by the Spirit of God, and held there. That fact of guilt, to a soul thus compelled to face it, is like a live coal to a naked eyeball.

Moreover, the worst of it is that conscience, if left to itself, never finds an adequate remedy. It never teaches a sinner how he may gain deliverance from sin or suffering. It never hints to him the possibility of deliverance from either. That is no part of its design. The design of conscience is simply to express God's law. Therefore, in a sinner's experience, its working is to express the evil of transgressing that law. Its legitimate work is to pour out upon a sinner burning and indignant accusations of guilt, of folly, of dishonor, of degradation, of moral defilement, of offensiveness to the holy universe, and of exposure to the wrath of a holy God, and — leave them there.

2. The destructive working of sin in a sinner's experience is further seen *in the fact that sin tends to develop sin.* Like all other forms of character, sin grows. Never for an hour is it at a standstill. No soul can live in eternal infancy. One sin begets another sin. Nothing else in nature is so prolific. One sin roots itself in the soil of character, and spreads itself outward, and lifts itself heavenward defiantly. Sin penetrates the underground of character, and forms there hidden enormities and unconscious depths of passion. A man of long experience in sin is always a worse man than he seems to himself to be. The day of judgment is to be a day of fearful surprises and overwhelming revolutions in self-knowledge.

Sin full-grown defies law because it is law ; resists restraint because it is restraint; contests authority with God because he is God. Says Cain, as depicted by Lord Byron in colloquy with Lucifer, "I bend to neither God nor thee." Lord Byron knew whereof he affirmed. This is the legitimate heroism of sin.

Sin runs to passion; passion, to tumult in character; and a tumultuous character tends to tempests and explosions, which scorn secrecies and disguises. Then the whole man comes to light. He sees himself, and others see him, as he is in God's sight. Those solemn imperatives and their awful responses, " Thou shalt not," — " I will," — " Thou shalt," — " I will not," — make up then all that the man knows of intercourse with God. This is sin in the ultimate and finished type of it. That is what it grows to in every sinner, if unchecked by the grace of God. Every man unredeemed becomes a demon in eternity.

3. The destructiveness of sin is still further seen *in the apprehension of its discovery, with which the consciousness of guilt is always more or less painfully attended.* Our souls are so made as to tremble at the thought of detection in wrong. This is often quite distinct from the fear of other suffering.

A burglar, not long ago, entered and rifled the contents of an unoccupied dwelling at the seaside. He ransacked the rooms from attic to cellar, and heaped his plunder together in the parlor. There were evidences that there he had sat down to rest, perhaps to think. On a bracket in the corner stood a marble bust of Guido's "Ecce Homo," Christ crowned with thorns. The guilty man had taken it in his hands, and examined it. It bore the marks of his fingers. But he had replaced it, and *turned its face to the wall*, as if he would not have even the cold, sightless eyes of the marble Saviour look upon his deed of infamy. Be it so, or not, there is in every human soul an instinct of concealment of sin, of which that act is a truthful emblem. The instinct of hiding clutches at every act of wrong-doing, and would bury it forever from the vision of pure eyes. The first act of the first sinner, when the fact of sin grew into his consciousness, was to hide himself at the sound of God's voice in the garden. Never till then had it been needful that God should ask, "Where art thou?" Thus human nature anticipated all through earth's history the craving for a hiding-place. Thus it foreshadowed the last prayer of the last sinner: "Rocks and mountains, fall on us, and hide us from the face of Him that sitteth on the throne!"

But what is the effect of this craving for concealment on a sinner's life? It dooms him to moral solitude. It shuts him into the society of his own outraged conscience. He must bear the torture of an inevitable Nemesis alone. That sometimes goads him by the sheer dread of detection to forestall it by confession, that he may be rid of the torment of anticipating it. Do not the history of suicide in this world, and the records of tribunals of human justice, confirm this working of the law of conscience?

These bodies of ours are so made as to be allies of conscience in this thing. They are sometimes all aglow and quivering with the signs by which this fear of detection in wrong discloses itself to the beholder. An eminent jurist in England, after long practice at the bar, said that he was awestruck by the machinery for the discovery of falsehood which God had constructed in the muscles of the human countenance. The human face, he said, was the most honest thing he had ever found in man. If every thing else bore the mask of perjury, he said, there was an involuntary muscle in one of the lips, which he had never known a witness to be able to control in the act of giving perjured testimony. The labial muscle, true to the hand of Him who made it, would start and vibrate at the thrill of the fear of detection, in the soul which crouched at bay behind it. So impossible is it, in the last extremity, for a guilty being to suppress its dread of discovery as a distinct and positive source of suffering in the experience of sin.

4. Once more, the destructiveness of sin in the experience of the sinner is seen *in the foreboding of judicial and eternal retribution which is incident to sin*. No two ideas are more indissolubly joined

in the working of the human mind than these two of suffering and sin. "Sin — suffering; suffering — sin." To a logical mind it is inevitable to reason from the one to the other, even to the tracery of a hair in the proportion of effect to cause. "So much sin, so much suffering:" this is law. And again, "So much suffering, so much sin:" this is law. Think what we may of it, this is law. Job's friends were true to the law of nature in this thing. These two angels of despair have trodden the ages as a winepress. It is the natural working of an honest conscience, unrelieved by the grace of God, to weld these two things together in the forebodings of a guilty soul.

Hence, in the experience of sin, it is sheer nature to anticipate suffering. And eternal sin must involve eternal suffering: this is nature. Yes; "it must be so: thou reasonest well." By nature, as well as by revelation, the worm dieth not. It is not superstition to fear an eternal hell; it is not bigotry to believe in it and to teach it: it is simple nature acting out one of its involuntary and elementary instincts. The heart's throbbing is not more natural. A fearful looking-for of judgment is, sooner or later, in the order of nature, the fruitage of all sin.

Besides, the human conscience finds no end to it. Once a sinner, always a sinner: this is nature. Therefore, once a sinner, always a sufferer: this, too, is nature. Again we must say, think what we may of it, this is law. It is no peculiarity of the Bible. Priests have not made it so. The Bible is no more responsible for it than the Koran. It is an obstinate *fact* in the make of the human soul. It declares the doom of any and every soul, if left to itself to drag a history of sin behind it.

Consequently man the world over trembles at something. Guilt sooner or later makes us all cowards. We are naturally afraid of God. We dread our own immortality. Who knows what is to come of it? We are afraid of death. Who has ever got an answer from the awful silence beyond? An English general of unquestioned courage confessed that he always trembled at the first boom of the cannon in battle. He feared it as much in his fiftieth fight as in his first. Do not such moments of standing eye to eye with death, and trembling at the booming echoes of eternity, occur in the lives of the best and the bravest of us?

But why? Why should a man fear death? A caterpillar does not fear the chrysalis through which it passes to a thing of beauty. Ah! but we are not butterflies. We are souls. We are images of God. Our dread of death, of immortality, of God, is the hammer of a deathless conscience falling on the anvil of eternal right, with the power of an almighty will in the arm that wields it. Woe to any thing that lies between!

An honest conscience, then, can never point a

man to himself for peace. It never tells him to look within for that. It shuts him in to his despair, and leaves him there. This is all that nature can do for him. If there is no other source of hope, he "goes out," like Cain, "from the presence of the Lord," to return no more. The *twin serpents* are the companions of his solitude, forever and forever.

From this review of the working of sin in the experience of men, two things become obvious:—

It is reasonable that a sinner should inquire anxiously, " What shall I do to be saved?" No man has any reason to be ashamed of anxiety for the salvation of his soul.

Equally obvious is *the preciousness of the work of Christ.* Christ becomes a reality to us, only by being felt to be a necessity. He *is* a reality only because he is a necessity. Here our thought should culminate,— in the preciousness of Christ to lost souls. Yes, lost! No other one word expresses so truthfully the condition in which Christ finds us all. Lost to virtue; lost to the respect and trust of the holy universe; lost to the benignant operation of conscience; lost to self-respect, to hope, to peace, to the conscious blessedness of being; lost to the complacent love of God,— the past all guilt, and the future all despair!

It is to such a being, to a crowded and forlorn world of such beings, that Christ gives himself. He gives himself to blot out the past. Oh, to blot out the past! We know little of ourselves if our experience has not taught us the need of that. We know as little of Christ's work for us, if we have not experienced the reality of that.

Yet how tame is language to express that experience! Are there not hours in which we can only adore in grateful silence the love of which we cannot speak? If we would speak, do we not fall back upon some such simple speech as that of those lines which have already been the solace of multitudes on death-beds, —

> "Just as I am, without one plea,
> Save that thy blood was shed for me,
> And that thou bid'st me come to thee,
> O Lamb of God, I come!"

AVOWED ENEMIES OF RELIGION.

After this did Sennacherib, king of Assyria, send his servants to Jerusalem (but he himself laid siege against Lachish, and all his power with him) unto Hezekiah, king of Judah, and unto all Judah that were at Jerusalem, saying, Thus saith Sennacherib, king of Assyria, Whereon do ye trust, that ye abide in the siege in Jerusalem? Know ye not what I and my fathers have done unto all the people of other lands? Were the gods of the nations of those lands any ways able to deliver their lands out of mine hand? Who was there among all the gods of those nations that my fathers utterly destroyed, that could deliver his people out of mine hand, that your God should be able to deliver you out of mine hand? And his servants spake yet more against the Lord God, and against his servant Hezekiah. — 2 CHRON. xxxii. 9, 10, 13, 14, 16.

THE enemies of religion are of two sorts. The enmity of one class is concealed from expression in words. It is often accompanied with professions of respect. It is covered by outward virtues. It may not be distinctly known to the conscience of the man himself. The enmity of the other class is open and avowed. The Christian religion is caricatured and libelled, and thus denounced. Its claims are ranked with those of obsolete mythologies. Religion itself in any form is pronounced to be the dream of superstition or the craft of priests.

148   STUDIES OF THE OLD TESTAMENT.

This second class of enemies to the cross of Christ are very strikingly paralleled by the character and deeds of the Assyrian king. He did and proposed to do by the sword, what they do and propose to do by tongue and pen. A very truthful picture of the one may be seen in the narrative of the other. Let us, then, read the character of modern hostility to Christianity in that of Sennacherib and his marshals.

1. The first thing which attracts our notice is *their boastfulness.* The Assyrian monarch evidently had no mean opinion of himself. "Know ye not," he says, " what I and my fathers have done?" "We are big men. We have great armies. We are flushed with victories. We do not know what it is to be beaten. Think twice, good people, before you presume to contend with me. Am not I the great and noble Sennacherib, successor to Nimrod the mighty, the victor in a hundred battles, who have put my foot on the neck of kings?" Such is the strain in which this Assyrian fellow swaggers at the people of the living God.

Hardly could a more truthful picture be drawn of the open enemies of God in every age. One thing is always characteristic of them, — they know how to brag. Self-conceit is their most obvious quality. They are rich in brass. Their claims are astounding to one who has not learned their loud policy. Voltaire predicted with brazen effrontery that Christianity would be defunct in twenty-five years. He claimed that he and the encyclopædists of France had written it to death. Yet to-day, after a century has gone by, the copies of the Christian Scriptures circulated in France alone, papal though it be, are numbered by hundreds of thousands every year, while the booksellers say that no other works lie on their shelves so long as the once-famous works of Voltaire.

It is a favorite device — one cannot call it argument — with the enemies of the gospel, to claim that it is obsolete. The world has outlived it. Like other superstitions it has had its day. The Old Testament especially is the object of this braggart strategy. "Does anybody believe that stuff now?" said a very young lady to a friend not long ago. "The world made in six days? Joshua stopping the sun? Jonah and the whale, and all that? Ha, ha! I thought that intelligent people had got over that." Probably she would have found it no easy matter to give a reason for her denial of the faith of her fathers. But her flippancy was the fruit of the loud-mouthed assertions of infidelity that the Old Testament *is* defunct.

Any lie persisted in may gain the force and momentum of a truth. These naked denials of biblical facts constitute in our day a very large share of the capital of infidelity. Science, it is claimed, has disproved the Mosaic cosmogony, at the very time when scientific men are finding out that there is a mysterious coincidence between the Mosaic and the geologic records. The testimony of the Book and the testimony of the rocks agree to such marvellous extent that unchristian scientists are beginning to inquire *where Moses got his information.* Moses somehow knew what it has taken science four thousand years to discover.

The *growth* of Christianity, it is declared, has ceased, and it is far on in the process of its decline; at the very time when secular historians are lauding it as outweighing all other civilizing forces put together.

The *intelligence* of the Christian system is denied: it is claimed to be only fit for children and fools; at the very time when it is commanding the faith of a larger proportion of the thinkers of the race than any other system known in history.

Christian *missions* are pronounced a failure, at the very time when they have made Christianity a power which the nations respect and idolatry fears over more than half the world. Cannibal tribes are transformed into fit allies of the most renowned empires and most enlightened republics on the globe, in less than half a century, by the preaching of a few men who went forth to their work amidst the world's mingled compassion and derision, — compassion for their fate, and derision for their folly; and yet the attempt to Christianize "happy and contented idolaters" is declared an antiquated blunder.

This, I repeat, is the policy by which the enemies of the Christian religion expect to browbeat its friends out of their faith. This policy is very old. Our religion has outlived a great many developments of it. First it was astronomy; then it was geology; then it was Chinese and Indian history; then it was Egyptian chronology; then it was flint arrowheads and stone hatchets; and now it is evolution and the correlation of forces, and so on, — which infidelity has declared to *have been* the death-blow to Christianity and the annihilation of its sacred books. The claim is not a prediction, not a conjecture, but a declaration of historic fact. The thing is done. The Christian system is defunct. All that the world has to do with it in future is to smile at the comedy, and learn wisdom from the blunder. It is in vain that we point to the achievements of our faith now in progress, and claim that it is a very lively thing for a dead thing. There is a class of "advanced thinkers" who will have their way about it. They ring the changes on the old story, — that the Christian religion is obsolete, and belongs henceforth to the historic mythologies. "Philosophers" and "seers" and "liberal thinkers" talk of Confucius and Zoroaster, and Moses and Mahomet, and Jesus and Socrates, — all in a breath, as if they were of equal authority, and all alike ciphers in the "Church of the Future."

It is related of an ancient king, that having vanquished his rival in battle, and taken him captive, he confined him in a cage, from which he was led out in chains daily, and compelled to bend to the ground at the saddle-bows of his victor, who used his prostrate body as a riding-block to assist him in mounting his horse. Like that is the imperious spirit with which the avowed enemies of Christ treat his claims to their faith.

2. A second feature by which this kind of hostility to religion is characterized is *its special animosity to the ministers of the gospel.* It is noticeable that the bragging Assyrian does not address his appeal chiefly to the Judæan king and his official representatives. His attempt is to stir up revolt among the populace, by appeals to their superstition and their fears. The official head of the kingdom and his subalterns are treated with contempt. They " spake yet more against the Lord God, and *against his servant Hezekiah.*" As the head of a theocratic kingdom, Hezekiah was the chief official representative to his people of the true religion.

Again and again is this hostility to the ministers of religion displayed by its open foes. The people are exhorted to revolt against " the priests." The popular name which infidelity gives to Christianity is " priestcraft." In every large community in which enmity to the gospel is openly professed, is to be found a class of men who are pre-eminently minister-haters. Their ridicule and denunciation are specially aimed at the clergy. No other class of men receive at their hands such severe measure and uncandid judgment. The human frailties of ministers are the butt of their satire. The fall of a minister, they never let the world hear the last of. That good-nature which the majority of civilized beings extend to men of other professions, is often denied to ministers. Lawyers, judges, physicians, merchants, teachers, journalists, may depend upon a fair hearing and a genial look from these men; but they are porcupines to ministers. When will the enemies to the popular theology of New England have done with Cotton Mather? When will the opponents of the Puritan faith, throughout the country, have done with the Salem witchcraft, and the whipping of Quakers, and the banishment of Roger Williams? Will the world ever accept the truth about the Connecticut Blue Laws?

The clergy, who are held responsible for all the moral blunders of their age, are the most roundly abused of men, living or dead. It is a sign of the general excellence of their character, and a sign, too, that infidelity fears them, that, with such concentration of the world's shafts upon them, they exist at all to-day, as a class respected and loved by anybody. No thanks are due to religious liberalism, that their characters are safe anywhere. What does communism say of the Christian clergy? What did it *do* to the humane and godly Archbishop of Paris in 1871?

3. Avowed enmity to religion is often characterized also by *the plausibility of its reasonings against the destiny of Christianity.* Sennacherib was a shrewd fellow. His speech to the Jewish populace was a very cunning specimen of demagogical oratory. His argument was a very plausible one. His facts were true. He and his fathers *had* been mighty men. Their arms had been crowned with success. The nations cowered before them. The gods of the nations had been as helpless before their conquering legions as so many bullocks. Reasoning upon the facts in the light of no other than the pagan theology, Sennacherib was right. His conquest of Judæa was a foregone conclusion.

"Were the gods of those nations any ways able to deliver their lands out of mine hand?"

"No."

"Who was there among all the gods of those nations that could deliver his people?"

"Not a god."

"How much less shall your God deliver you out of my hand!— you, little petty Judah, not so large as the least of my provinces!"

"True: it is a fact."

Such must have been the colloquy between them, carried on by the Jewish hearers silently and with sinking hearts. On the pagan theory of the gods, and in the light of recent history, the Assyrian monarch had the best of the argument by all odds.

So it often seems in the controversy between religion and its avowed enemies. They often seem to make out a strong case of it. Much can be plausibly said against religion and its friends. Facts can be made to seem conclusive against them. Real difficulties are found in our faith, which no wise man will pretend that he does not feel. Science discloses facts which require modifications of our interpretations of the Scriptures. Astronomy gave a fearful shock to popular faith in the Bible — simple as it seems to us now — when it revealed the fact that the sun did not move around the earth. As simple will seem the explanation of other scientific mysteries by and by; but they are none the less startling at the outset, for that.

The ministers of religion, too, are but men, often weak men, sometimes wicked men, always imperfect men. The assaults of infidelity upon them often seem very plausible. Religion itself has to bear the brunt of them.

Specially do the confident predictions of the downfall of Christianity often seem morally certain. The philosophical proof alone of this is unanswerable. It is the great marvel of history, that such a religion as ours can hold its own at all in such a world as this. By all the laws of human evidence by which men prognosticate the future, the Christian religion ought long before this time to have disappeared from the face of the earth.

Its temples ought to be now antiquarian ruins, of which curious travellers should be ferreting out the history and the meaning. The Scriptures ought now to be stored in antiquarian libraries, not read or cared for by twenty men in a generation.

On purely philosophical grounds, the enemies of our religion are right in their assurances of its speedy overthrow. The balance of natural probabilities is never in its favor. The great forces of this world are its allied foes. Crises have occurred in its history, in which persecution has been backed up by wealth, by learning, by the prestige of antiquity, by civil law, by public opinion, and by bayonets, — by all the great forces which sway society and compact empires; and thus allied, it has borne down — upon what? Upon armies bristling with steel? upon Ehrenbreitsteins and Cronstadts? No: upon a handful of poor men and friendless women and little children, who had no weapon of defence but prayer!

Many times has the success of persecution seemed to be a foregone conclusion. Many times has its success appeared to be an accomplished fact. It has laughed at failure as a bugbear. It has burnt up the handful of men, women, and children, as the Duke of Alva did in the Netherlands. The people of God even have often thought their case a hopeless one. "We trusted that it *had been* he that should have redeemed Israel." Oh, yes! We did trust, but our trust is disappointed. Our enemies have triumphed. Our cause is hopeless. We can only lie down and die.

Periods sometimes occur in which scepticism becomes for a time the popular *mood* of a nation. Infidelity is greeted by the controlling minds of the time. Universities and royal societies nurse it. Elegant literature dandles it. Poetry sings it. The sciences pay tribute to it. Fashion coquets with it. Philosophy crowns it. Wealth builds temples to it. Philanthropy and liberty bring incense to it from afar. Even to the friends of Christ it seems as if every thing were going against them. Society seems to have run mad with unbelief. What was Paris in 1789, and again in 1871, but one vast lunatic-asylum of unbelievers? At such times, to worldly wisdom it is the right thing to prophesy the speedy extinction of Christianity.

4. The history of the avowed enemies of Christ is characterized by *the certainty, the suddenness, and the unexpected means of their disappointment.*

Somebody made very short work with Sennacherib. One night was time enough to answer his gasconade at the people of God. One verse is all that the historian thinks necessary to tell the story: "The Lord sent an angel which cut off all the mighty men of valor." One angel of the Lord was a match for the Assyrian battalions. The mighty men were not looking for such a re-enforcement to their enemy. That was the last thing they dreamed of. That destroying angel, be it a pestilence or a storm, or a miraculous apparition, was the "angel of death" to a hundred and eighty-five thousand of the Assyrian hosts before morning.

The fame of that mysterious event spread quickly around the world. It became the symbol of all sudden national deliverances. It lives thus to our own times. Isaiah's triumphant description of it is read every year in the churches of Moscow, on the anniversary of the salvation of the Russian Empire by the celebrated retreat of the French army in 1815. The opening watchword of the Judæan song of triumph, "God is our refuge and strength," has furnished the inscription over the greatest of Eastern churches in Constantinople. It is the foundation, too, of the noblest national hymn in Western Europe, — Luther's far-famed "Ein' feste Burg ist unser Gott."

An English poet has celebrated the event in words so full of the old Hebrew spirit as to deserve citation here: —

> "The Assyrian came down like a wolf on the fold,
> And his cohorts were gleaming in purple and gold.
> . . . .
> Like the leaves of the forest when summer is green,
> That host with their banners at sunset were seen:
> Like the leaves of the forest when autumn hath blown,
> That host on the morrow lay withered and strown.

AVOWED ENEMIES OF RELIGION. 159

> For the angel of Death spread his wings on the blast,
> And breathed in the face of the foe as he passed;
> And the eyes of the sleepers waxed deadly and chill,
> And their hearts but once heaved, and forever grew still!
>
> And there lay the steed with his nostril all wide,
> But through it there rolled not the breath of his pride.
>
> . . . .
>
> And the tents were all silent, the banners alone,
> The lances unlifted, the trumpet unblown;
> And the might of the Gentile, unsmote by the sword,
> Hath melted like snow at the glance of the Lord."

The history of our religion develops often a similar phenomenon in God's dealings with its avowed and boastful enemies. They are sure to be disappointed in the result. *Something* keeps Christianity alive to-day, centuries after, by the logic of its foes, it ought to have been dead and buried. Something makes it grow and thrive. It never had a deeper hold upon the world's faith than now. Never before did its friends look out upon a more resplendent future.

Often the local triumphs of our religion occur suddenly. A revival of religion changes the mood of a community in a month. Corrupt institutions like slavery fall suddenly, and by unlooked-for agencies. Times of apparent decline of religion are often times of preparation, in which great principles are secretly taking root; and at length they start up and grow as acknowledged powers of Christian truth. The *visible* progress of our religion in the world is commonly by sudden leaps and revolutionary changes. A single angel from the living God works out results at which both friends and enemies of truth stand amazed.

Sometimes in private communities it is the angel of Death. Opposers of religion are sometimes removed at a moment so critical, that men cannot but silently put the two things together. By ways of his own, God achieves his eternal purposes.

> "God moves in a mysterious way,
> His wonders to perform."

A TALK WITH YOUNG PEOPLE ABOUT JOSIAH.

Josiah was eight years old when he began to reign, and he reigned in Jerusalem one and thirty years. And he did that which was right in the sight of the Lord, and walked in the ways of David his father, and declined neither to the right hand nor to the left. For in the eighth year of his reign, while he was yet young, he began to seek after the God of David his father: and in the twelfth year he began to purge Judah and Jerusalem from the high places, and the groves, and the carved images, and the molten images. — 2 CHRON. xxxiv. 1-3.

IT is a noticeable fact, that the histories in the Old Testament, of kings and other great men, tell us so much about their youth. Where they were born; who their fathers and mothers were; what happened to them in their childhood; how old they were when they began to reign; the fact that some of them were boy-princes, — just the things about them which interest young people in them in all ages, — are thought worthy of a place in the word of God. We may reasonably take it as a sign that God feels special interest in children and youth, that he has constructed the Bible so.

The story of Josiah is not so well known as those of Samuel and Joseph; but it is told with the same kind of zest, and is as full of lessons most valuable to the young.

1. It shows, among other things, that *a child may become a Christian very early in life.* He was but fifteen years old when he is spoken of as "seeking the God of his father David." That was the first that people knew of it. But probably he had been a prayerful boy long before that. He had been a king then for seven years. If he had been a wild wayward youth, this would probably have been mentioned.

There is no more difficulty now in a young person's becoming a Christian than there was in the case of King Josiah or of Samuel. When youth has been spent in sin, sin has become a habit. The habit of sin is quick in forming. Once formed, it is a powerful hinderance to conversion. The natural and easy way for a child is to *grow up* a Christian, so as never to remember the time when he was not one.

Nathan Dickerman is sometimes spoken of as an unnatural boy, because he gave evidence of being a child of God at the age of four years. Many have thought that that had something to do with his early death. "All the good boys die early," it is said of Sunday-school books. The books may not all be what they ought to be, but Nathan Dickerman's early piety was just the most natural thing in the world. We shall probably have many such cases as the millennium ap-

A TALK ABOUT JOSIAH. 163

proaches. That is the true way of coming into the church, — growing into it from earliest years.

2. The narrative of this young king shows also that *young persons may become Christians without the excitement of a revival.* I have heard children wish that a great revival would occur, and carry them into the kingdom of Christ in a whirl of excitement. They think it would be so much easier, if everybody else were beginning to serve God. If their companions were ready; if George and Henry and Mary and Julia would join them; if there were a great stir about religion; if people were talking of nothing else, — it would appear so natural then to do as others do! If Mr. Hammond, the children's preacher, would come, and hold a series of meetings, and form a child's church, with a covenant which a child could understand, some imagine that they would be among the first to rise and say, "I will obey Christ."

Perhaps they would; yet they might not be any nearer heaven than now. People are often deceived in a revival. None are more likely to be so than young people, who know little of their own hearts. In a great excitement, Satan often tries to make one think one is a Christian falsely, so as to escape real conversion.

Besides, often the great test of our willingness to obey God is, whether we are willing to do it *alone.* To do what others do *not,* may be the very thing that God requires. If we truly love God, we should obey him if we were the only persons in the world to do it. We should do it all the more for being alone. If the dear Saviour had no other friend, would you desert him, and leave him with none? It would be heroic to stand by him then. This Josiah did when he began the reformation of his kingdom: he stood absolutely alone. He started the revival by being the first convert.

The great question is an individual one. Daniel Webster once said, that, of all the subjects of human thought that had ever occurred to him, this was the greatest and the most impressive, — "the *personal* relation of the soul to God." Salvation lies between each single soul alone and God alone. Each one of us must die alone. Each one must go into eternity alone. Each one must be judged alone. It will matter very little then what others have done. God will inquire of you what *you* have done. Why should you wait for others, or they for you? Waiting is a perilous thing when God says "Now." "To-morrow" has ruined a great many souls.

3. King Josiah's conversion shows that *a young person may become a Christian just at the time when the pleasures of the world are the most attractive.* He was at an age when the world is fresh and new to a young man. He was a king. This world is a beautiful place to a youthful prince who has health and wealth and leisure and princely com-

panions to make it such. One could be happy in such a world forever.

The young often plead it as an excuse for neglecting to obey God, that they are so young; the world so new; so many of their associates are irreligious; and they have so much to make a worldly life enjoyable. Not so did the youthful king reason. Life could scarcely look more attractive to anybody than it did to him. He might have made one long holiday of it. That was the fashion of the time. Nobody thought it necessary to be religious but a few old gray-haired prophets. It would have attracted no notice, and nobody would have blamed him, if he had lived a life of respectable neglect of God. But he loved God. He wished to please God.

The happiest life conceivable in this world is the life of one to whom God gives the innocent enjoyments of youth, and adds to them the deeper joys of religion. There is no contradiction between them. God enjoys the sports of the young more than they do, if only they love him. Who is it that makes the lambs skip, and the birds sing, and the squirrels chirp, and the bees hum? Their pleasure is all pleasure to God.

4. The story of Josiah shows, further, that *a child may be a Christian without being unmanly or unwomanly*. Boys sometimes imagine that religion will take the spirit all out of them. I have never heard girls say this, but I suspect they have often

felt it. I have heard it said that "the pious boy is the milksop of the family." If this is true, it is very strange that King Josiah did not turn out so. He began to be religious very early. We do not know that he was ever any thing else. But even at the age of nineteen years he was a great reformer. Reformers are not apt to be milksops. Did anybody ever call Luther a milksop? The pope did not call him so. He found him such a lively opponent that he could think of nothing to do with him but to burn him. When Luther entered the hall where the Diet of Worms was in session, one of the ablest military commanders of the age tapped him on the shoulder, and said, "Monk, monk, thou art on a passage more perilous than I ever knew on the bloodiest battle-field." Such milksops are the great reformers of the world.

King Josiah was one of such. He did for his country and age what Luther did for Europe. He was the most energetic man in his kingdom. We sometimes say of a very bright youth, that he is the life of the house. King Josiah was just that. He made things lively for everybody. Judah never had a more spirited and gallant prince. Had he lived in the middle ages, he would have been renowned for all chivalrous virtues. Did you ever read of the "Knights of St. John"? In all their innocent exploits, King Josiah would have been one of them. He put down the bad men of the realm, right and left, most valiantly. Not one of them dared to insult him.

At last he lost his life by courageous exposure in battle, though warned beforehand not to risk it. The whole nation mourned for him as one of the bravest monarchs they had ever had; and this after a long reign of thirty-odd years. If his piety had made a prig of him, would not his people have found him out in that time? Yet they loved him and mourned for him, much as our country loved and mourned for President Lincoln.

Let me tell you how the idea has come about, that religion makes a boy a chicken-hearted fellow. It is just because religion cultivates certain *still* virtues. Benevolence, purity, reverence, meekness, charity, the forgiveness of injuries, and such like, are required by the law of Christ. A young man who becomes a Christian will not swear, nor quarrel with his companions, nor break the sabbath, nor insult his teachers, nor sing ribald songs in the streets, nor brag about fighting everybody. In a word, he will not be a *rowdy*, but a gentleman. Therefore he will be nicknamed "milksop" by rowdies. That he must expect. It is an honor to be nicknamed by rowdies. He should remember that all that religion requires of him in this respect is that he cultivate and practise the very virtues which are necessary to make a gentleman. The very highest type of character which the culture of the world has ever conceived of is that of a *Christian gentleman*. And that is precisely what religion makes a young man. By the way, have you ever thought what is the meaning of this word "gentleman"? It is only a *gentle-man.* That is, a man possessed of the quiet and passive graces, just those which the Christian religion teaches. Wickedness always tends to rudeness, to violence, to angry and turbulent passions, to loud and profane speech. The noblest culture of the world unconsciously supports the Christian religion in teaching a boy that he must be a *gentle-man.*

I have heard of an ignorant boy who was very fond of fighting, who, when he was asked who was the person in heaven whom he most wanted to see, sang out, at the top of his voice, "Goliath!" He thought the Philistine giant was a much more respectable man than Solomon. So long as we number among the godly men of the world such men as David and Solomon and Josiah, and St. Louis of France, and Edward the Sixth of England, and Gustavus Adolphus, and William of Orange, and Washington, and Lincoln, we have no reason to fear that our religion will make us chicken-hearted. When that takes place, the world will have to find some other name for its finest characters than that of *gentle-man.*

5. The history of this ancient prince suggests also that *one who becomes a Christian early in life is likely to become a better man than one who first lives through a career of sin.* He is likely to be a more consistent Christian. He will probably have fewer faults to get rid of, and fewer habits which his piety must break up.

A TALK ABOUT JOSIAH. 169

It is remarkable that through the whole of Josiah's long reign, — one of the longest in Judæan annals, — not one wrong thing is recorded of him. Doubtless he had faults, and did wrong things; but not one was important enough to be mentioned in the Bible. Other great and good men are mentioned in the Scriptures, who were very inconsistent. They did some very wicked things. Some of them had long periods of wickedness, in which they displeased God exceedingly, and had to suffer for it. The Bible is very honest about its great men. It does not conceal their faults, nor make them out better than they were. But of King Josiah it has not a thing to say with which God finds fault. The only important mistake recorded of him was that in which he lost his life by fighting with the king of Egypt. The narrative appears to indicate that God incited the Egyptian king to warn him that he would lose his life if he went into the battle. But there is no evidence that he knew that the warning came from God. He thought it was the notion only of his enemy. He determined that his enemy should not outwit him in that way. Therefore, like the brave man he was, and the father of his country, he plunged into the thickest of the fight, and died as brave soldiers love to die. Except that one mistake of excessive bravery and patriotism, not a thing is recorded of him that went wrong.

This indicates that as he grew up to manhood

he had a very symmetrical character. He was a great and good man *all around*. This was the natural result of his early piety. Other things being equal, those become the best men and women who spend the largest portion of their lives in serving God. They have the least to *undo*, in consecrating their lives to Christ, the fewest old sins to overcome, the least headway of sinful habit to get rid of.

In my boyhood I used to attend the church of the late Rev. Albert Barnes of Philadelphia. He used to preach, once in two months, a sermon to us children. We thought him the holiest man in the world. We used to call him "the beloved disciple," he was so like the apostle John. We did not believe that St. John was a better man. But I well remember his confessing to us, that, though he had then been a Christian for more than twenty years, he had not entirely got over certain wrong habits of thought and feeling which he had indulged in his youth. He lamented all his life that he had not given his heart to God in his boyhood. He said, that, if he had done so, he should have been a better Christian and a happier man.

6. The story of this good king suggests further, that *the way for a young person to become a Christian is to make a business of doing right*. Josiah's whole life was spent in setting things *right* throughout his kingdom. Before his reign every thing had gone

wrong. The worship of God was neglected. Idols were worshipped instead. The word of God was lost. The people had become so wicked as to have forgotten what God had commanded in the law of Moses. That was as if you and I should become so heedless of God's words as to forget the Lord's Prayer. The temple which Solomon had built with such magnificence was so neglected that cattle broke into it; and every thing was in a bad way.

As soon as the young king was old enough to understand the state of things, he set himself, and his ministers, and his cabinet, and his soldiers, and his workmen, to putting things to rights. He began early, and kept at it, and spent his life in it. Nobody else put him up to it. It was his own idea. We are told that he "covenanted to serve God with all his heart and with all his soul." This is what I mean by making a *business* of doing right. He started with the very first thing that he had to do, and *did it right*, and in order to please God.

Now, this is the true way to be a Christian. There is no great mystery about it. There is nothing in it which a child cannot do by the grace of God as well as anybody else. You can do it as well as I. God does not require you to go through any long season of unhappiness, in trying to feel as some others have felt in repenting of sin. You have only to do right in order to please Christ. That is religion, and that is the whole of it.

To a young child, religion consists very largely in obeying parents; running on errands pleasantly; speaking the truth; learning lessons faithfully; being respectful to teachers; being kind to playmates, especially the poor ones and unhappy ones; reverencing the aged; praying with the heart, instead of "saying prayers;" and doing all these things in order to please Christ, because he is good and has died for you, and you love him.

Take the very first thing you have to do; be it only to go for a glass of water for your mother, or playing a game of croquet with your sister, when you had rather play marbles than do either: do the thing that costs you something, and do it *right*, and do it because it will please Christ. Christ *will* be pleased with it, as truly as he was with Solomon for building the temple, or with Josiah for repairing it.

Then *keep* doing things right, and in order to please God, all your life. That is living a Christian life. It will be made up largely of little things. Christ has taken pains to say to us that he is contented with little services from us. A cup of cold water given in the right way shall not lose its reward. He notices little things more than he does great ones, because there are more of them, and everybody can do them. Make a business of doing them right, and he will remember it thousands and millions of years hence, and when he comes to judgment. Out of all the millions of people that will be there, he will call for *you*, and say, " Come, ye blessed of my Father."

AN ANCIENT MODEL OF YOUTHFUL TEMPERANCE.

But Daniel purposed in his heart that he would not defile himself with the portion of the king's meat, nor with the wine which he drank. — DAN. i. 8.

THE Old Testament often seems as if it were inspired especially for young men. The lesson before us answers with singular pertinence the inquiry which every young man ought to ask and answer in a manly way: "*What stand shall I take respecting obedience to the drinking usages of society?*"

We talk of the *old* prophets. But at the time of which we now speak, this one was a very young man. He comes home, therefore, to every young man's level. He takes each one by the hand for a plain brotherly talk on a very stale subject. Let us listen and overhear the young prophet's counsel.

I. What were Daniel's temptations to abandon a life of abstinence from strong drink? Many a namesake of his may look into his own life for the answer.

1. He was tempted *by his youth.* He is sup-

posed to have been from eighteen to twenty-two years of age, when the question of abstinence became a practical one to him. He was at the age when appetite is strong, health good, principle weak, and experience not at all. A young man starts often on a life of self-indulgence by simply doing nothing, thinking nothing, caring nothing. He just prolongs into manhood the animal instincts of childhood. Before he knows it the mischief is done. We are all animals before we are men. Drinking is our first natural pleasure. It is for each young man to say for himself whether it shall be the last.

2. Daniel was tempted also *by the usages of his social rank*. He was a noble, probably of the blood-royal. It was the usage of his order to drink wine, and the best of it, and much of it. Probably then, as now, it was the sign of a gentleman in the circle of society in which the young nobleman moved, to know good wine when he tasted it, to use it freely, and to enjoy the social hilarity of it without scruple. Oriental literature had its drinking-songs, like those of Burns and Thomas Moore. Babylon had its Fifth Avenue, its Chestnut Street, its Beacon Street, where the social aristocracy of the city discussed the contents of their wine-cellars, as did the guests at the marriage in Cana. It required not a little moral courage for a young noble of the royal stock of Judah to go to the metropolitan dinner-parties,

and leave his wine untasted. "An odd fellow, this young Hebrew!" his companions said. "Yes, indeed! Does the upstart Jew think to teach *us* what should be the habits of a Babylonian gentleman?"

3. Daniel was tempted *by the courtesies of official station.* He was in training for the first office in the realm. He encountered the same temptation which a young man would now encounter if he were invited to dine at the mansion of the French Minister in Washington. "If I have the honor of drinking the health of the beautiful and accomplished daughter of the Hon. Secretary Xerxes, shall I play the 'boor by refusing, for the sake of an absurd scruple about a glass of wine?" Such was the gist of the question which put the principle of the young Hebrew to the test. How many young Americans in official circles would have borne the trial?

4. Daniel was tempted also *by his professional prospects.* Few young men have ever lived who have had a more splendid opening before them, to a magnificent professional career, than the young prophet statesman had at the court of Babylon. He was noted for his manly beauty. His personal address was that of an accomplished nobleman. He was acquiring the ripest culture of the age. He had only to conform to the usages of the most select and refined society of the capital, to make sure of a career which should satisfy the utmost

ambition of an aspiring youth who was conscious that he had in him the making of a great statesman, and a leader of men.

The temptation was the same in kind with that which assails a young lawyer or physician in New York or Philadelphia, who has his own way to make in his profession, and who, if true to the principle of total abstinence from intoxicating drinks, must by his example reprove the very men on whose support he depends for professional success. Said one such, "A carriage and a conscience are expensive luxuries. In my profession one cannot enjoy both. I prefer to drive my carriage." So did *not* the young civilian at the court of Babylon.

More than one member of the American Congress has died a sot because he could not withstand this form of temptation. One member of the Supreme Court of the United States, of a past generation, was persuaded by his friends to resign his office, and retire to the practice of his profession in his native State, because he could not endure the peril to which the drinking habits of Washington subjected a man in his position. "Bodisco's wines are too much for me," was the lame apology of an intoxicated senator for his beastly appearance in the Senate Chamber after a dinner the night before at the mansion of the Russian minister. If report be true, more than one member of that honorable body now owe to the young men of the country a similar humiliating confession.

5. Daniel was tempted also *by his absence from home and native land*. The tour of Europe has broken down the principles, and broken up the habits, of multitudes from America. Paris is a volcanic vortex to scores of American medical students. One such, when his ruin was complete, beyond hope of recovery, used his medical knowledge as a means of reckoning how many years his broken constitution could bear the excesses to which he had become addicted. "I know," said he, "that I can enjoy life in my own way about so many years. I shall parcel out my fortune to last so long a time, and no longer. When my time is up, my revolver shall end all. No long decline for me. Dying is wretched business, and shall be soon over." Parisian life had given him both his habits and his ethics.

A young man does not know how much of the real grit of right principle he has in him till he goes away from home, and lives where nobody knows him; where he can live anyhow, and do any thing, and yet come silently back, and his old friends shall be none the wiser. Alas! many such young men have brought back seared consciences and hardened hearts, and habits of self-indulgence which have doomed them to a drunkard's grave.

Yet this form of temptation the young Hebrew statesman did not escape. He met it in its most urgent form. He was not only in a foreign land, in the Paris of the ancient world, in the court of a king, associating with corrupt young nobles and aristocratic pleasure-seekers, but he was a captive. He had no home. His own country, as an independent kingdom, was blotted from the map of Asia. Judæa was to Asia what Poland is to Europe, — nationally and politically it had ceased to be.

Polish nobles to-day, in the capitals of Europe, seek to drown their memory of their country's wrongs. If anybody could find palliation of intemperate habits, they can find it in their national misfortunes. Just that form of intense temptation young Daniel encountered at the age of twenty-one.

Put now all these things together, — youth, social usage, official rank, professional interests, absence from home and native land, and the mortifications of captivity, — and where, in modern life, can you find a case of stronger temptation to a self-indulgent and pleasure-seeking career?

II. Pass we now to observe what was the young nobleman's conduct in the trial.

1. He was true *to his faith in abstinence from the use of wine.* Let us not muddle ourselves here with irrelevant matters. Whether or not wine-drinking is a sin *per se;* whether or not a pledge to abstain is a duty; whether or not membership of a temperance society is wise; whether or not

wine is more innocent than rum; whether this, that, or the other is the wisest policy, — do not at all concern the point in hand.

The point is, that the young prophet had a principle of his own on the subject, and adhered to it. He believed, no matter why, that for him wine was a forbidden luxury; and he stuck to that conviction. He was not cajoled out of it by selfish interests nor by side issues. A remarkable thing about him is the absence of casuistry. He makes no attempt to hoodwink his conscience. He accepts it as a plain case. Duty settled, every thing is settled. He will be true to that, though the heavens fall. Not one of the inducements he had to twist his conscience awry, and create for himself an exceptional case, has a feather's weight with him. His friend and superior talks of the danger of losing his head. He retreats none the more for that.

Yet he does not bluster. He does not even say much of conscience. He does not fling his convictions in the face of his friends. He does not browbeat those who differ from him. Not a word appears which implies that he thought wine-drinking a sin in them. Heads shall be saved, and friendships kept intact, if it may be honestly done. It deserves emphasis, that, in fidelity to his own convictions, he did no violence to those of others. In becoming a reformer he did not cease to be a gentleman.

2. Daniel was true *to the education of his childhood.* His convictions were doubtless the fruit of early training. He is not ashamed of that. He indulges in no swagger about the bigotry of his father, and the narrow mind of his teachers. He does not plead that now he has come to manhood he must act for himself, and will not be bound by the usage of his father's house.

Young men sometimes break away from the temperate principles and habits of their youth on this plea of personal independence. They boast that they have attained to greater breadth of view than the fathers had. Ah, yes! breadth of view. "Broad views," I have observed, are but the gilded gateway to the "broad road." They remind me of the young man of whom I have somewhere read, who would no longer read the Bible which he had been taught to revere, "because," he said, "it has such a mess of Presbyterian bigotry in it." Daniel is gulled by no such nonsense. He will put his foot into no trap of self-conceit which Satan may set to catch the vanity of youth.

He has been educated to do *right*, and of that he is not ashamed. His conduct is clearly in contrast, and is meant to be, with the customs of the society around him. Jerusalem against Babylon: that is the gist of it. His father's house stands over against the court of the king. The training of his childhood is pitted against the corruption of the heathen capital. Jew against Pagan: when it comes to that, he stands manfully by the traditions of his own kindred and the home of his infancy. His silent soliloquy is, "Mine be the God of my fathers, mine the old songs of my country's faith, mine the prayers that my mother taught me."

3. He was true also *to the principle of temperance as a religious virtue*. The drinking customs of Babylon often meant more than they seemed to mean. They were saturated with the virus of idolatry. A Chaldæan dinner-party was a sacrifice to the gods of the kingdom, as were afterwards the social entertainments of Greece and Rome. If a state banquet were given at the palace, instead of inviting the young Hebrew to dine with the princes of the realm, the invitation would read in some such form as this: "His Majesty the King commands the presence of Belteshazzar at a sacrifice to Baal."

It became, therefore, a very essential element in the policy of the prophet-statesman, that it should be pervaded by the dignity of *his* religion. The idolatrous banquet at the palace must be met by the religious temperance of the guest. Thus Daniel practised temperance as a religious virtue, — nothing less. He put it on the basis of a religious scruple. "He purposed in his heart that he would not *defile himself* with the king's meat and wine."

Language cannot well express more truthfully the fundamental principle of the temperance reform. The virtue it inculcates is a religious virtue. It is a religious reform, or it is nothing. Its opposite involves moral defilement, to which no young man of lofty and pure spirit will subject himself. Pure manhood in this thing needs to respect itself with much of the delicacy of chaste womanhood. Both revere the sacredness of the human body. They treat it as the temple of God. Rarely do young men maintain their position as the friends of temperance on any less holy ground.

Said the Bishop of Calcutta, on the platform of a native society for the improvement of Hindoo morals, "If you wish to make any thing eternal, you must build it on the Christian religion. That is the only thing in this world that *is* eternal." He was right. No reform is worth its cost, which is not important enough to rise to the level of a religious duty. Make it that, to the consciences of men, and it will live. Make it less than that, and men may play with it for a day, but will never *build* it into any thing that can live to future ages.

4. The prophet also *calmly trusted the consequences of his procedure to God*. There is something sublime, as there always is in such phenomena, in the assurance of this youthful hero that he *may* trust the end with an unseen Power. He has only to do his duty amidst the intricacies of his lot, and an invisible Friend will care for the rest. He has no fear of losing his head. If he must lose it, be it so. There is another thing which he

fears more. He asks for but ten days, however, to show who is in the right. He will stake his chances on ten days of prayer. A short time often shows on which side of things God stands. The powers which prayer brings to the front often move quickly. God loves speed in decisions for him.

The great thing which a young man needs in a crisis of temptation is to declare for the right quickly. Leave no time for temptation to accumulate. Then intrust consequences to God. It often requires a great deal of character to do that; not only a religious principle, but a strong character back of that. To be content, in a crisis, with the single thought of *duty*, is one of the grandest things in history. Yet a child can do it. God never disappoints that trust. When a young man throws himself headlong into the sea of temptation, with only the one spar of duty to lay hold of, God is there to uplift and bear him over the billows. In grasping duty, he grasps a living and almighty hand.

There is an old book, yet extant in some of our libraries, which tells the story of an old man who was the warrior-poet of his tribe. He had seen much of life, and been conversant with many lands. He had stood in the cottages of shepherds and in the courts of kings: dens and caves were not unknown to his checkered career. The literature of his age was familiar to him: he had been no mean contributor to its treasures. At length when, near the end of his days, his countrymen gathered reverently around him to listen to the wisdom of the old soldier in the forms of Eastern song, he summed up the result of his long experience of the ways of God with men in these words: "I have been young, and now am old, yet have I not seen the righteous forsaken, nor his seed begging bread." When a young man is called to hazard something that is dear to him at the call of duty, he can find in all the literature of the ages no anchor that grapples more securely in the storms of life than this testimony of the old man of Mount Zion.

III. What were the results of Daniel's fidelity in his own experience? These must now be said in few words. By his temperance he gained a healthy body. It gave him athletic sinews and pure blood. It secured to him what many young men value more, — a fresh complexion and the look of manly courage. No blotches on his face blabbed of secret vices. His was a countenance before which a pure woman's eye would not fall. He gained also that "richest boon of a good man's life,"— an unsullied conscience. He slept and waked, and waked and slept, at peace with God.

In that brief trial of his youth, he laid the foundation of a robust, religious manhood. He laid then the train which led to a long and splendid career of courtly usefulness. The mysterious power which subsequently closed the mouths of lions for his safety began at this time to gather around his person. In this early and brief fragment of his life, he settled the future of his professional career as a prophet of the living God. Those ten short days secured to him a place in the world's history, in which he is destined to live in the grateful and reverent affections of mankind forever. Who cares now for the Chaldæan monarch and his haughty court? They live to-day in the world's memory only because this young Hebrew seer has condescended to speak of them. As one of the authors of the word of God, and one of the great actors in the history of God's Church, he is to live while time lasts. Men of all ages will inquire for him in heaven. They will point him out, one to another, as the interpreter of the "handwriting on the wall." Children there will seek him out as "the man of the lions' den." The redeemed of all times will revere him as one of God's great ministers and chosen friends.

The foundation of this magnificent destiny, extending into two worlds, was built far back in those few days — not longer than a boy's holidays — in which the character of the young man was proved, and his principles tried, as a friend of temperance and the child of conscience.

THE LOST BIBLE.

And when they brought out the money that was brought into the house of the Lord, Hilkiah the priest found a book of the law of the Lord given by Moses. And the king commanded Hilkiah, and Ahikam the son of Shaphan, and Abdon the son of Micah, and Shaphan the scribe, and Asaiah a servant of the king's, saying: Go, inquire of the Lord for me, and for them that are left in Israel and in Judah, concerning the words of the book that is found: for great is the wrath of the Lord that is poured out upon us, because our fathers have not kept the word of the Lord, to do after all that is written in this book. — 2 CHRON. xxxiv. 14, 20, 21.

THE apocryphal historian of Judæa extols the memory of King Josiah as being "sweet as honey in all mouths, and as music at a banquet of wine." This Oriental eulogy is due largely to his agency in the recovery of the *lost Bible* of his kingdom.

Few more remarkable events can happen in a nation's history than the loss of the sacred book of its religion. Nations have deliberately abandoned the faith of their fathers, and adopted a new religion. But the loss of a religion from a nation's *memory*, so that its sacred book, when recovered, is welcomed as a novelty, is an event seldom if ever paralleled outside of Judæan annals.

The remedy of such a loss is justly regarded as the great event of the reign of Josiah.

Scarcely can a more sublime scene for a great historic painting be conceived of, than that of this youthful monarch, standing amidst the assembled magnates of his kingdom, and leaning against a pillar of the temple, while he reads to the astonished crowd brought together by the news of the discovery, the whole book of Deuteronomy, from beginning to end.

No wonder that the devout monarch rent his robe, and the people were overwhelmed at the anathemas which they had brought down upon themselves and their children by permitting the religion of their fathers to pass utterly out of the traditions of the kingdom.

We may make an instructive use of this scene, by inquiring *what we should lose if we should part with the Christian Scriptures and with all the institutions and blessings for which we are indebted to them.* We appreciate a treasure most thoroughly when we have lost it. We realize the value of a fortune, of health, of a friend, of a good name, most keenly, when they have gone from us. " Blessings brighten as they take their flight."

Infidels often charge us with childishness in loving our Bible as we do. " Why care so much for a *book?*" they say; " why revere so devoutly an antiquated volume which the world has outlived, whose fables children marvel at, and wise men laugh at?" The best answer to these things is to imagine that the world had lost "the book," and had lost with it all that it has given to mankind. Would that be a thing for wise men to laugh at, and wits to jeer at?

1. In the loss of the Bible and its fruits, we should lose *the knowledge of the true God.* History proves this beyond reasonable dispute. An unanswerable argument for the fact of a revelation from God, is the fact that the world *needs* one to assure it that there *is* a God. God must *speak*, or man does not find him. Men are like lost children searching in the darkness for their father and their father's house. He is searching for them too; but they do not recognize him till they hear his *voice*, calling their names in the wilderness or in the fog. When we are taunted with the fact that ours is the religion of a *book*, the answer is sufficient, that mankind needs a book to keep alive in the earth the knowledge of a spiritual and personal God. Blot out the Bible and its effects from the world's history, and we fall back by slow but sure gradations into the condition of the most debased of African tribes. Serpents and monkeys become our deities. We are fortunate above many of our fellow-men, if we rise so high as to pray to the golden globe of fire which rises every morning over our eastern hills.

2. By the loss of the Scriptures and their results from the knowledge of mankind, we should lose,

sooner or later, *our institutions of benevolence*. Benevolence on any large scale, and in the form of permanent institutions, and for all classes of mankind, is a biblical idea. Hospitals, asylums for the insane, retreats for the fatherless and for widows, and the thousand kindred forms in which charity to the unfortunate and the poor has expressed itself in Christian lands, are among the trophies of the Christian Scriptures.

The sporadic and fitful attempts of charity to express itself in heathen institutions do not deserve mention by the side of the beneficent records of Christianity. A heathen philosopher, once visiting the country, was conducted through many of our public buildings. When he had received our hospitality, and was about to return, he said to a friend, "Your prisons, and your dungeons, and your scaffolds, and your armies, I understand: my country can outdo you in such things; but your orphan-asylums and old men's homes astonish me, and your homes for old women would seem to my people ridiculous."

Even De Tocqueville, coming from a papal country, where the Scriptures are padlocked, was amazed to see charity extended in this Bible land to criminals. Our societies for reform of prison discipline were a novelty to him. Said he, "In my country, once a rascal, always a rascal. You do things differently." Yes, we do things taught by the example of Him who ate with publicans and sinners.

It would be an exaggeration to say that charity, in the form of almsgiving, cannot exist without the Bible. Heathenism has often made that a condition of salvation. Hospitals and houses of refuge are not unknown to Buddhism. But charity systematized, charity extended into all the sinuosities of social life, charity founded on the principle of the common brotherhood of man, cannot exist where the Bible is unknown. The brotherhood of man is a biblical idea. It is revealed from heaven. The popular mind of the race has never originated it when left to work out its own theories of society. Moreover, even such forms of benevolence as do exist in heathen lands do not stand the assaults of human selfishness, in the long-run, unless re-enforced by the religion of the Scriptures. The drift of heathen civilization is downward, not upward. Nothing but the word of God has restorative force enough, as a humanizing and civilizing power, to arrest that decline, and give to the principle of benevolence a permanent and sovereign sway in social institutions.

A pamphlet lies upon my table, of more than three hundred octavo pages, which contains little else than the *titles*, with brief explanatory notes, of the charitable institutions of the city of New York alone. The combined literatures of Greece and Rome never produced a volume like that. They never could. The ancient republics contained in their palmiest days no material for the production of such a work.

Infanticide, the exposure of superannuated parents, slavery, human sacrifices, and cannibalism, are ultimately the usages and institutions in which human nature expresses the drift of its selfish instincts when untaught by a revelation from God. It requires only time enough for those instincts to come to their maturity in a finished depravity, to work out the extinction of organized benevolence. Over against such results, we now find more than ten thousand charitable associations in the single State of New York. Every one of these would pass out of existence if we should strike out of the civilization of the Empire State the Christian Scriptures and their natural products.

The State of Massachusetts has expended more than two millions of dollars upon a single asylum for the insane. Banish the Bible from the schools and the homes and the *character* of Massachusetts, and in less than the life of three generations we should have here a people to whom taxation for such a purpose, beyond the need of caging the insane like tigers, would be denounced as tyranny. It is not yet a hundred years since the insane and wild beasts were treated alike in some parts of Europe. Strike out the Bible from our *history*, and every such asylum, and all kindred institutions with which the State is dotted from Berkshire to the sea, would give place to institutions and customs of organic selfishness, and ultimately of barbarian cruelty. The spirit of the Bible must be in the homes of a people, and its sacred words on the lips of their children, and its humane spirit in their hearts, before society and government can develop themselves on any large scale in the forms of organized benevolence.

Conceive, then, of a sovereign state in which, from end to end, should be found not one hospital; not one retreat for the insane; not one home for friendless and aged women; not one asylum for orphans; not one house for abandoned children; not one infirmary for incurable invalids; not one asylum for the blind; not one refuge for fallen women; not one school for the deaf and dumb; not a spot where Laura Bridgman could find a friend; not one institution for the care of idiots; not one provident society; not one almshouse; not one sanitarium for the cure of inebriates; not one association for the employment of street-Arabs; not one mission-school; not one sewing-school; not one society for the protection of emigrants; not one home for sailors, not one for soldiers; not so much as one little "Shoe and Stocking Society," such as once honored the North End of Boston,—conceive, I say, of such a sovereign commonwealth, and, in place of these, imagine it dotted all over, as it must be, with prisons and penitentiaries and scaffolds and pillories and whipping-posts, with rum-shops at every corner to furnish material for these grim expedients of justice; and you have some faint picture of what Massachusetts would be if she could have existed at all without the infusion of the Bible as her life-blood into the framework of her civilization.

3. In the loss of the Bible and its fruits, we should sooner or later suffer the loss of *our institutions for popular education*. Here, again, it would be untrue to say that heathenism is of necessity and always barbarism. Culture has existed without a revelation from heaven. Schools are not the product of the Bible only. But it is beyond question, that *popular* education is of biblical origin. Besides the impotence of heathenism to *sustain* even such culture as it creates, and to prevent the relapse of the race into barbarian ignorance, it is a truism that other than Christian religions build themselves on the ignorance of the *masses*. Even Greek and Roman civilization — the most brilliant that man ever framed without the aid of a revelation — knew no such thing as that which we understand by the education of the people. Cicero was perhaps, on the whole, the most enlightened and liberal statesman the world ever saw outside of the biblical circle of civilization. Yet no man has ever lived in whose mind was more profoundly rooted the aristocratic idea that education is for the few, and ignorance for the many; ease and leisure for the few, and toil and slavery for the many.

Heathenism everywhere assumes that the people exist to be governed, and that, to be governed well, they must be kept in ignorance. Voltaire betrayed his want of the biblical idea of culture in saying, "The people must have bread and amusement. But do not teach them to reason."

The drift of culture without the spirit of the Bible in the heart is seen in the hostility of the ancient governor of Virginia to the spirit of New England, which he expressed by thanking God that Virginia had no free schools, and praying that she might never have such "pests." That is human nature when educated in ignorance of or hostility to the spirit of the Scriptures.

Witness the testimony of the Romish Church. Locking up the Scriptures and fighting free schools go hand in hand. The Vatican has one of the most costly libraries in Italy; but a traveller who visits it sees only the blind oaken doors which shut it in. Education there is for the few only, and for them only by permission of authority. So it is the world over. The free Bible and the free school stand and fall together.

Add to this the putrescent tendencies of society, when not counteracted by the antiseptic power of Christianity, and the inevitable sequence of the loss of the Scriptures must be the loss of all that should deserve the world's respect in popular education. Imagine, then, the State of Virginia, with the prayers of Sir William Berkeley answered. Picture to your fancy the Old Dominion with not one schoolhouse in all its broad domain;

not one college or university or seminary for either sex, which should be open to free access from the lower and middle classes of society. Imagine that it had not one newspaper printed in the mother tongue; not one free library; not one popular lyceum; not a popular lecture given on either side of the Blue Ridge from year's end to year's end; not an institute of teachers ever held there; not one printing-press for the publishing of popular information; not so much as a Farmer's Almanac seen anywhere; not a speech delivered from the stump to enlighten the people in their civil duties; not a post-office open to any but dignitaries of the State; not a telegraph-pole erected within its borders: in a word, give back the old Virginia plantations to the savages from whom they were bought or plundered, and you get some dim idea of what a great country like ours would be if the word of God were expunged from its history. That our land is any thing better than that to-day, as the abode of popular science and general culture, we owe to the fact that Sir William's prayers were *not* answered, but a free Bible was left to work out its own fruits in a free press and free schools.

4. By the loss of the Scriptures and their creations, we should sooner or later part with *our institutions of civil liberty*. History shows that the great charter of freedom in the world is the word of God. The great free nations of the earth are

the great Christian nations. And of those the most free are the great Protestant peoples who keep God's word clear from the dominion of priests. The institutes of Moses are marvellously imbued with the principles of our own republic. The principle of our town-meeting is found in one of the provisions of the Mosaic code for the government of the people. A volume has been written to show the republicanism of the civil constitution given by the great Jewish lawgiver. Where, think you, did Thomas Jefferson get the idea of democratic government which he embodied in the Declaration of Independence? From an obscure Baptist church in the backwoods of Virginia.

Yes, if you would imagine a land from whose civilization the Bible and its products are wholly lost, and faded from the people's memory, you must conceive of a land of slaves and tyrants; a land without a written constitution; without a declaration of independence; without a bill of rights; without trial by jury; without an elective franchise; without a jurisprudence framed to guard the liberties of the citizen; without courts and tribunals organized and managed in the interests of equal justice; without legislatures representative of the popular will; without one of that galaxy of institutions and unwritten laws which we deem the glory of our Republic. Every one of these we owe ultimately to the Christian Scriptures.

My space fails me. It was my purpose to show

that the loss of the Bible and its fruit from the world would involve the destruction of *peace* and its attendant blessings; that *war* would become ultimately the chronic condition of society; that the modern idea of the *family* would be lost; that the institution of *marriage*, as we understand it, would cease to be; that *woman* would be reduced to servitude; that *home* would lose its holy meaning; that *infanticide* would be restored; that *human sacrifices* to infernal deities would become the prevalent form of religious service; that protection against desolating *pestilences* would become impossible; that *cannibalism* would live again; and, in a word, that the tendencies of the human race to *barbarism* in its most brutal forms would be revived, and that its natural career would be towards its own *extinction* on this globe. The whole earth would be subjected at last to the destiny which overtook and had well-nigh overwhelmed the savage tribes of this Western continent when Christianity found them two hundred and fifty years ago, and towards which the best civilization of the world was drifting when Christ was born.

One of the great poets has portrayed the scene in which *light* should be banished from the universe. He describes the blotting out of stars and moons and suns; this earth still wandering in the blackness of the universal dark. He pictures men living by watch-fires. They burn up their forests, their cities, their homes, their temples, and all holy things, to create a light by which to see each other's faces, and get warmth against the growing intensity of cold. Commerce dies; its once famous marts crowded with the products of distant lands are forsaken: not so much as a blade of grass grows in the deserted streets. Ships rot in their harbors. Sails which have whitened every sea flap idly in the dead night air. Men grow wolfish in the universal woe. They curse each other, and gnash their teeth, and howl for one ray of light. Mothers turn savagely upon their youngest-born. No love, no family, no home, survives. Temples of religion there are none; and, as for God, men have forgotten but to curse him and die.

Gradually the whole globe becomes depopulated. It rolls in space without inhabitants save two survivors, and they are mortal foes. They scrape together a fagot and a few dried leaves, and blow them to a blaze, that they may once see each other's faces. Then with one look of frenzied hate, and a shriek of maniacal fury, impotent to wreak itself except upon itself, they expire. So human history is ended. Not a hand is left to roll up the map of nations.

"The world is void,
Seasonless, herbless, treeless, manless, lifeless,
A lump of Death."

Such a world would this earth become if the

light of the word of God were once put out, and all that it has done to illumine and elevate and civilize and refine and redeem mankind were blotted forever from its history. Such would be the consequence of a final and irremediable loss of the Bible.

GOOD MEN WHO ARE NOT CHURCHMEN.

And Jeremiah said unto the house of the Rechabites, Thus saith the Lord of hosts, the God of Israel: Because ye have obeyed the commandment of Jonadab your father, and kept all his precepts, and done according unto all that he hath commanded you; therefore thus saith the Lord of hosts, the God of Israel: Jonadab the son of Rechab shall not want a man to stand before me forever. — JER. xxxv. 18, 19.

THE foregoing title expresses in brief the leading practical idea which we derive from this biblical fragment about the Rechabites. Opinions may not unreasonably differ about this singular people. But as I understand the scriptural notices of them, they were not Israelites by birth, nor included in the covenant of God with his peculiar people. Yet they were good men. They recoiled from the wickedness of the world around them. They sought, as men are in all ages prone to do, to find protection in ascetic vows.

They saw, for instance, that intemperance was a great and damning vice: therefore they vowed that they would drink no wine. They correspond very nearly, in that respect, to the modern societies of " Good Templars" and " Sons of Temperance ; " that is, they were pledged to the practice of total abstinence; yet were not, by virtue of that vow, members of the church of God.

They saw, also, that the great cities of the world were the chief centres of corruption: therefore they vowed to live forever in tents. Their ancestor and founder, Jonadab, was a Bedouin Arab, as we should call him. The desert was his home, and the tent his dwelling. It was a vow of the sect to live so forever.

They observed, also, that the possession of fixed property was a great temptation to men. They would therefore have none of it. Every man bound himself not to own a house, not to buy a field, not to till a vineyard. Like the Dominicans and others of the Romish Church, they took the vow of poverty, so far as these forms of worldly estate were concerned. They would escape sin by fleeing from temptation. That was their principle.

These three things seem to have been the creed of the sect: to drink no wine; to own no fixed property; to dwell in no permanent abodes. Their organization as a tribe was clearly an attempt to live a purer life than the world around them, by cultivating the simple tastes and habits of herdsmen, living in tents, wandering wherever they could find pasturage, being much in the open air, and at night sleeping under the resplendent skies of Arabia.

But what have these ancient "Good Templars" to do with the mission of Jeremiah to the kingdom of Judah? Just this, and no more: they are used as a means of reproof. They were faithful to their vows: the Jews were not. They adhered to the religion of their fathers: the Jews did not. They were practically better men and women than the average of the world: the Jews were not. They kept themselves clear from the corruptions of the great metropolitan cities: the Jews did not. They practised the virtues of temperance, of plain living, of frugality, and the kindred virtues of country life: the Jews had given themselves up to the extravagance and the idolatrous vices of the great capitals. So far as we know, they worshipped the true God: the Jews had become so corrupt as to worship a calf, a goat, a lizard, any thing that anybody worshipped; they followed the fashions in their religion.

The prophet therefore *uses* these "Good Templars" as a means of shaming the men of Judah for their wickedness and apostasy. I do not understand that he means to give the divine approval to them as a sect; or to set the divine seal upon their vows, as necessary to holy living; nor even to defend their total abstinence. It is a stretch of biblical authority, to make this fragment an argument for the divine authority of temperance-societies. Other scriptures may support them, but not this one.

The prophet seems to say to the apostate Jews, "Look, you renegade people of God, look at these

Rechabites! Are you not ashamed of yourselves? They have not had half of your privileges, but they outdo you in right living. They are consistent with their professions. They stick to their vows. They live up to the light they have. You do neither. Therefore, by the authority given me by the living God, I tell you that God will bless them, and will curse you."

This I take to be the simple purpose of this introduction of the Rechabites into the word of God. In a nutshell, the design is *to reprove bad men in the Church by contrasting them with good men out of the Church.* The value of such a fragment in the Scriptures for practical use in all ages may be seen by a brief notice of the following hints: —

1. The popular criticism upon the Church is true: "*Better men are out of it than some men in it.*" There are bad men in the Church, and very imperfect good ones. Men profess religion who will cheat in a trade, who will lie to cover the cheat, who will take a false oath to bolster the lie. Name almost any crime that quick-witted depravity can invent, and doubtless it has been committed by some professed child of God. Prudent merchants refuse credit to a man who pleads his standing in the Church as a reason for giving him credit. Christian ministers, too, have done their full share of deeds which have pierced the heart of Christ. The chivalrous and manly virtues in some men overbalance the Christian graces in

some other men. There are "Good Templars" and "Odd Fellows" and "Free Masons" who make their fraternities substitutes for the Church, and we cannot say that the substitution is not plausible.

When the world charges us with these contrasts, we admit them. When we are asked what we have to say for ourselves, we answer nothing in defence of such men, but bow our heads in shame. We can at best echo St. Paul's lament, and "tell you even weeping, that they are enemies to the cross of Christ."

2. *The contrast between apostates in the Church, and good men out of it, is an exception to the general fact.* As the Rechabites of old were a small and exceptional sect, no fair representative of the heathen world, so now the good men who are not churchmen are not a fair specimen of what men naturally become who live out of covenant with God. As in the Jewish Church there were men and women who were not apostates, so there are multitudes in the Christian Church now who do not deserve the charge that they are no better than other men. The apostates and hypocrites on the one side, and the good men who are not churchmen on the other, are both exceptions to the general law. It is but fair to admit this. It is but just to claim it.

The very fact that the alleged contrast attracts attention and provokes satire is proof of this. If it were the general law, that the Church makes men scoundrels, and that irreligion makes men the pattern of all the virtues, the charge of inconsistency would disappear. If it were the natural drift of things that clergymen should be adulterers, thieves, liars, drunkards, the fact would be accepted as the legitimate fruit of their profession. They would, as a class, stand in public esteem where blacklegs do now. Public opinion rests at last upon the *facts*. In the West-India Islands and in some parts of South America the Romish priesthood have, *as a class*, fallen into debasing vices. They drink, they lie, they swear, they gamble, they brawl, they are licentious. They suspend mass to attend a horse-race. These things are so common that public sentiment accepts them as the usual accompaniments of the priestly function. They have long since ceased to excite remark. No hue-and-cry is raised when a priest is guilty of these things. The popular proverbs run thus: "As bad as a priest;" "As drunk as a friar;" "As tricky as a Jesuit," and so on.

Such would be the popular judgment the world over, before long, if the fact of clerical depravity were universally true, or if it were generally true that Christian ministers are no better than the average of men. It is not true, and the world knows it. It is a calumny which no man who is not innately and thoroughly dishonest and mean will charge upon the clerical office. The man who has lost faith in such a body of men and women as now compose the Protestant Church of Christendom, and large portions of the Catholic Church, must be a man who has lost faith in himself. His loss of trust in their virtues springs from the loss of consciousness of those virtues in his own heart. He believes no better because he *is* no better.

3. *The concessions which Christians make to cynical critics of the Church need often to be qualified by loyalty to the brotherhood.* There is a virtue in loyalty to one's guild, which truth and justice sometimes call to the front.

There is a tone of criticism of the Church which sounds very candid, and very faithful, and very independent of clanship, which, after all, is unmanly and mean, simply because *it is not true.* Underneath it, there is a truckling to the malicious judgment of the wicked. The faults of Christians are exaggerated. The numbers of the hypocritical are overrated. Guilt is assumed on insufficient evidence. Evidence which a jury would scout is deemed sufficient to condemn a professor of religion. Such accusers do not face the accused like men. They will swell a secret into common fame; yet, when summoned to bear witness, they skulk.

All nations have a proverb about "the bird that fouls its own nest." All honorable men respect loyalty to one's own. The conditions of

Christian living in this world are such as to call for large practice of this virtue. No other body of men are so sure of receiving unjust judgment as Christians are. To belong to the Church of Christ is to be a mark for cynics to hawk at, and for vultures to peck at. In simple fair play, the Church needs the magnanimous graces among its own members. Does not everybody know a professing Christian who has the inconsistencies of his brethren at his tongue's end always, and their excellences never? That brother should look into "trades-unions" and "Masonic lodges," for a lesson in loyalty.

I have somewhere read a legend of a wretched man, one of nature's monstrosities, the tip of whose tongue was a snake's head. In his sleep the hideous reptile lay coiled within; but his breathing was a low and ominous hiss. When he woke, and attempted to speak, the monster thrust itself out in wavy vibrations, hissing, biting, stinging. A fitting symbol this of men who can never find a good thing to say of the Church of Christ. Inspired imagery resembles the revolting legend: "They have sharpened their tongues like a serpent; adder's poison is under their lips." Shall brethren in Christ thrust such venomous fangs at each other? When tempted to misanthropic judgment of a Christian brother, remember the snake-headed tongue. The truth is that conscious hypocrites in the Church are comparatively few.

GOOD MEN WHO ARE NOT CHURCHMEN. 209

And what of ministers of the gospel? I have elsewhere spoken of the inconsistencies of the Church and her ministry with sufficient fidelity. May I now offset it with a bit of testimony? True, it is interested testimony: but no other can be founded on knowledge of the facts; it must pass for what it is worth. For more than thirty years I have known the clerical profession as no man can know it who is not in it and behind the scenes. With more or less of personal intimacy, I have known nearly two thousand preachers of the gospel. I know their aims, their motives, their methods, their weaknesses, their policies, their secrets; for every profession has its honorable secrets and its wise policies. And my conviction is that there is not another body of men living, of equal numbers, the record of whose life, public and private, will bear scrutiny so well as theirs. The testimony which the Earl of Shaftesbury publicly gave to the character of the American missionaries in Western Asia, in 1860, "they are a marvellous combination of common sense and piety," is true of the great body of Protestant ministers whom I have known. Out of the whole number, but five have made a wreck of moral character. Of what other profession or guild, equal in numbers, and chosen at random, can that be said?

Similar is the testimony which any man who knows the facts will bear respecting the great body of the Church. When men claim that the Church as a body has done nothing to lift the standard of human virtue, that Christians as a whole are no better than other men, it is wrong by silence even to give in to the calumny. It is but just to the living and the dead to protest that *it is not true*. The facts of life do not bear out such sweeping censures. To concede the justice of them is treachery to men and women of whom the world is not worthy. It is a confession that our Lord did not know *how* to lift this world up into redeemed and regenerated life, when he planned the doing of it by the agency and example of the Church. It is a confession that *his* work, through eighteen centuries of churchly life, has been a dead failure. Who believes this, except those who wish to believe it?

4. *The virtues of good men who are not churchmen are due largely to the salutary influence of the Church upon them.* The Rechabites owed their knowledge of the true God to the Jewish people. Their virtues were due to their association with that people, not to their knowledge or practice of heathenism and its fruits. Similar is the teaching of history in all subsequent ages. The *virtues* of the world in their finest growth live upon the *graces* of the Church.

A cannon-ball, in its course through the air, moves, with a velocity only less than its own, a certain bulk of the surrounding atmosphere. That "wind of the ball" is sometimes strong enough to knock a man flat. When you stand close to an express-train of cars at full speed, you feel the same phenomenon. Within a certain distance, the space around a body in quick motion is filled with its momentum, and the air moves as it moves. Similar is the moral power of the Church of Christ over multitudes who are taught its principles, who know its creed, who witness its example, and whose infancy was fashioned by its ordinances. They feel its *restraining* power when they do not bow to its *saving* power.

Christian *ideas* govern the public opinion of the world to-day, though spiritual religion is by no means in the ascendant. It takes but a small minority of earnest believers to carry with them the speculative belief of a large majority. So nations populous and mighty are nominally Christian to-day, because they contain a nucleus of spiritual Christians. These keep alive the Christian religion as a power of restraint, of culture, of refinement, of civilization, of virtue, to multitudes to whom it is not yet a power of salvation. That such men are what they are, they owe to the living faith that is in the Church. They owe it to godly mothers and praying fathers, and Christian wives, and the recollections of their own Christian childhood. That among them are found Christians in heart who are not such by profession, they owe to the more positive and consistent ones, who do not fear to profess before the world the faith they cherish in secret. The Church of Christ achieves thus a vast amount of unacknowledged conquest.

The moral virtues in their ripened forms live in this world on the life-blood of the Christian graces. Christian sap is flowing through the whole tree of European and American civilization. Profound and far-reaching is the principle, " Ye are the salt of the earth."

5. While God blesses goodness and the right wherever he finds them, he *still depends for them chiefly upon the Church which he has created for all time*. History, in this old Judæan line, seems to turn aside for a moment to salute respectfully these ancient sons of temperance. Yet it speedily returns again to the old channel of the Church of God. No sect is taken as a substitute for the Church. God does not abandon his people, and take up Rechabites in their stead. He knew his own mind when he founded the Church, and said to Abraham, " In thee shall all the nations of the earth be blessed."

Traces are still found, in the wilds of Arabia, of the descendants of the ancient tribe of Jonadab, in fulfilment, as it is believed, of Jeremiah's prophecy. But how little has been the Rechabite influence on the world! We have to search biblical antiquities to find it. The world knows nothing of its history. Turn to a secular historian, and you find that a few lines are all that he thinks it necessary to give to this ancient sect; and those only because it is mentioned in the Bible. Compare the article "Rechabites" with the article "Christianity" in any good encyclopædia. Just such is the *proportion* of the good that is in the world to the good that is in the Church, in respect to the strength of each as a spiritual power, and their value to the coming ages.

The great stream of civilization and redemption has flowed down the ages of the past, not through any accidental and wayside canal of Rechabite or Masonic virtue, but through the great river-bed of the Christian Church. Here are the living fountains. Here are treasured the truths which the world most needs to know. Here are garnered the promises which gild with golden radiance the world's future. The hope of all coming time is in this Church of the living God.

6. The principles we have thus briefly glanced at suggest that *heaven is full of surprises for those who reach it.* Said an aged clergyman when drawing near to that world, "I expect to find there some who I have never thought would get there; and I expect to miss some whom I have supposed to be sure of it." Yes, surprises of this sort await us. Not every one that saith, "Lord, Lord," shall enter there. Many who did not say "Lord, Lord," will be found to have given the cup of cold water to some disciple. God only knows his own. He will gather them from the

four winds. Not one will escape his eye. He will need no church-records to inform him who they are. He will need no marble monument to tell him where their dust reposes. He will need no epitaph to tell him what they were. Not one bruised reed of virtue will be broken, not one flickering flame or buried spark of grace put out, by his avenging hand, in the great day. Yet it is to be a "great and terrible day." Fearful disappointments will be found there. Said a devout but trembling saint on his death-bed, "There must be some tremendous examples held up to the universe: what if I should be one of them!"

It becomes us all to walk humbly before God. Professions of religion cannot save us. Vows in the Church or out of it cannot save us. The contrite and believing *heart*, — this, and this only, is the place in which God dwells. This is his living temple. This is more to God than the pillar of fire and the pillar of cloud, — more than the Shechinah and the holy of holies. This is more to Christ than church and clergy and sacraments. "I heard a great voice out of heaven saying: Behold, the tabernacle of God is with *men*, and he will dwell with them. God himself shall be with them, and be their God."

INTERTWINING OF GOD'S PLANS WITH THE PLANS OF MEN.

> But the army of the Chaldæans pursued after the king, and overtook Zedekiah in the plains of Jericho; and all his army was scattered from him. Then they took the king, and carried him up unto the king of Babylon to Riblah in the land of Hamath; where he gave judgment upon him. And the king of Babylon slew the sons of Zedekiah before his eyes: he slew also all the princes of Judah in Riblah. Then he put out the eyes of Zedekiah; and the king of Babylon bound him in chains, and carried him to Babylon, and put him in prison till the day of his death. — JER. lii. 8–11.

THE title of one of the most useful of modern sermons is, "Every Man's Life a Plan of God." The story of the Judæan captivity brings to view, as every other great event in history does, these two distinct lines of purpose, — the line of God and the line of man. To effect God's will in the fulfilment of ancient prophecy, some one man must take the leadership of the people. Some one man must head their downfall. Some one man must lead their sad procession into bondage. Some one man must suffer there the barbarities of ancient warfare; must see his children slaughtered one by one before his eyes; must suffer worse than death in the loss of his own sight; and must die at last a dethroned prince, a childless father, a blind old man, in an enemy's country, and in a dungeon. Yet the great wheels of Providence moved on calmly and relentlessly, crushing out that one life as if no being in the universe cared for it. No friendly ear seemed to hear the death-cry of the victim.

Of the many truths which the passage before us teaches, *this mysterious intervolution of the plans of God with the plans of men* will seem to some minds the most impressive.

1. The enclosure of the plans of men within the plans of God is such that *commonly men appear to be left very much to themselves*. This unfortunate prince, whose lot it was to close the line of independent monarchs on the throne of Judah, does not appear to have been overruled by any visible network of divine purposes, any more than the humblest beggar in Judæa. When the historian came to record his life, the record would naturally run, "Such are the chances of war; such is the fate of unfortunate princes in barbarous times."

Yet all the while a plan of God enveloped him, which touched and checked at all points his plans, directed his working to God's ends, and wrought out over and around him a chapter of universal history, which was to concern the world in distant ages, and nations yet unborn. Nearly twenty-five hundred years have come and gone since then;

more than seventy generations have lived and died; yet on the first Lord's Day of the month of May, this year, millions of people in many lands, making a belt around the globe, were pondering the fate of that blind old man in the dungeons of Chaldæa.

Such is the sublime involution of every human life with the purposes of God. So noiseless is his working, that, when men are defeated, his agency is not forced upon their notice. They need not see him if they choose *not* to see him. Commonly they do not see him. They say of their misfortunes, "Luck was against me." "Such are life's chances." "We've lost the game."

2. In leaving men to themselves in the forming and working of their own plans, *divine control does not prevent the occurrence of very shocking catastrophes.* Look at this miserable old Jew. His contemporaries saw nothing unusual in his fate. That he should be vanquished in war, that he should be caught in his flight, that he should be marched into captivity, that he should be thrown into a dungeon, that he should be chained like a wolf, that his children should be butchered before his eyes, that those eyes should be gouged out by the hangman, and that he should linger out his wretched old age, a blind captive and a disgraced prince, who could only long to die, excited no surprise. That was the usage of the age. Such were the contingencies of royal birth, and the

chances of war. He knew it beforehand. The world said of him, "He took his chances, and they ran against him. He played his game, and lost it. He probably would have treated his royal foe in the same way if he had gained it."

But we read the story with blood running cold. It shocks our sensibilities, that any human being, the most insignificant in the universe, should be thus overridden and crushed by the spiked wheels of states and empires. We marvel that God should suffer such things. Can there be a God, we ask, who can permit such useless torture of a lone old man? A society of atheists once published a card on which were printed these words: "What becomes of God's omnipotence, if he *would* have prevented suffering, and *could* not? What becomes of his benevolence, if he *could* have prevented suffering, and *would* not?" Sure enough, without a revelation we cannot explain one such scene in the drama of one human life.

Yet such is the darksome way in which God moves. Verily thou art a God that hidest thyself. He seems to keep himself aloof, in awful seclusion from human woes, as if the sight of them were either too much, or too little, for such as he. I go forward, but he is not there; and backward, but I cannot perceive him. Does not every-day human life often force the cry of Job from white and trembling lips?

INTERTWINING OF GOD'S PLANS.

A young husband and wife start on their bridal tour. Loving and loved, their hearts open to all living things, the future seems to be one long golden age. In a few hours, they are dragged, with charred arms infolding each other's lifeless forms, from the ruins of the wrecked train at Ashtabula, and their bridal tour is ended.

A factory building, five stories high, falls to the ground just after seven hundred men and women and children have begun their afternoon task. Through the oily crevices of the ruins, fire creeps and hisses and leaps, and coils itself around its helpless victims, like a swift, mad serpent. I stand by what were just now living and chatting men and women, and children whom mothers "kissed good-by" an hour ago. I see them now, still and stark, arranged in ghastly order on the floor of the city hall. I observe that the arms of many, burned to the blackened bone, have been thrown up to fight off the flames from their roasting faces. Oh! can there be a God in the same world where such things are? If there be one, is he not such as Elijah laughed at? Does he not tarry, talking with somebody? Is he not hunting? Is he not on a journey? Is he not asleep? Oh! who, what, where is he? Oh that I knew where I might find him!

A man was once drawn out insensible from the ruins of a railroad-train after a collision, he the only living one of twelve. He said that when he came to himself, the first thing he noticed was a bluebird singing merrily in a hazel-bush near by.

On the field of Shiloh, where four thousand wounded and dying men lay in their blood all night, the blue and the gray side by side, one of them looked up reproachfully to the cold stars. "Why," thought he, "do they not veil their faces? They seem to wink to each other at this scene of agony, as if it were the *dénoûment* of a comedy."

Yes, God does seem to leave men to their fate at times, as if death-throes were no concern of his. All happy things at such times appear to mock human agony with a ferocity all the more unbearable because it is so still and so beautiful, yet so cold-blooded. Individuals are left to work out their own ruin. Tempters do devil's work on the young and the unwary. Innocent ones suffer with the guilty. Nations trample out nations in the rage of their huge passions. The millions are dragged under by the pride of one. Helpless women and little children are the victims. The great wheels crash into and crumple up the little wheels. Happy homes give place to battlegrounds. Wheat-fields grow rank, fertilized by human blood. Artillery thunders in cemeteries, and ploughs open graves. "Glorious victories" are but the pretty name of hell. So human life goes on. This is *history*. It was in view of such possibilities in every human life that DeQuincey said, "Death we can face; but, knowing what life is, which of us is it, that, without shuddering, could, if consciously summoned to it, face the hour of *birth?*"

3. Yet the plans of God *envelop and use the plans of men with more than motherly tenderness for every man, every woman, every child.* In infinite pity he looks down upon man, woman, child, one by one. The remoteness of his hiding is only the measure of his love. All the mystery springs from the fact that his melting eye looks so far ahead, and his soft hand reaches down to the roots of suffering, so far beyond our sight, or even our will to see.

This truth in its fulness we owe to the Bible. Through the whole range of the Old Testament this idea runs, — that God is a personal and faithful Friend to every one who will be *his* friend. "*My* God;" "*my* Rock;" "*my* Fortress;" "*my* Deliverer;" "the God of Abraham;" "the God of Isaac;" "the God of Jacob;" "Abraham, the *friend* of God;" "Moses, my *friend;*" "ye are as the apple of mine eye;" "I will do them good with my whole heart and with my whole soul." Do we venture to say, "Our Father"? He responds, "As one whom his *mother* comforteth, so will I comfort thee."

The New Testament declares the same with yet more intense significance. A fond mother dotes over the glossy ringlets of her boy: he finds them among her garnered treasures when, in strong manhood, he has followed her to the burial. But God, with the affairs of a boundless universe on his mind, has found time to do what was never done by young mother to her first-born in the leisure of the nursery, — to number the very hairs on his head. We have but a faint conception of that love which belongs to creatorship and redemption. God only knows the love of God.

Taking this key from God's word, we can unlock the whole mystery of life, so far as suffering is concerned. To the eye of a good man, it is not so much the greatness as the minuteness of God's love which overwhelms him. Scientists claim that the microscope has revealed more of the wonders of nature than the telescope. So it is the microscopic look into human life which reveals the most marvellous loving-kindness of God.

Let any man once give faith to the biblical thought of God as his personal friend, and carry it back to the review of his own life from infancy up, and he will find the evidence of divine love to him, as if to him only, coming in upon his soul like the flood of many waters. The invisible hand is seen in such things as these, — I select at random from one life only, — an old song which the mother sang in the Sunday twilight; a tree, a stream, a lake, a mountain, which were more than friends to our boyhood; a certain chance interview with a friend, which was rich in lifelong results; a speech heard on a certain festive day; the sight of the great man who first awakened great aspirations within us; the sight of the good man who first made religion a reality to us; a certain book come upon at hap-hazard; a certain sermon heard long years ago, or one sentence in it, or the text only; the death of the college friend which first made heaven a fact to us; the mild reproof of a certain saintly woman; the first lesson in practical astronomy; a Christian hymn sung somewhere in the mountains; the gift of a rosebud from a hand now still forever; a certain conversation with a stranger in the cars; last words from a mother's death-bed; a certain prayer heard when homesick in a foreign land; the mysterious delays which prevented us from embarking on board the ship that went down at sea; a look at the Bay of Naples; an hour in the Colosseum at Rome; the hour spent in the "closes" of Edinburgh where Chalmers labored; the Lord's Supper at Lucerne.

Can we not all recall *similar* events and circumstances, some of them too minute to mean much in the rehearsal, but which have been so inwrought into our subsequent life that we cannot but break forth sometimes into a carol of thanksgiving at the thought of them? I know a man whom the perfume of mignonnette in the month of August moves to ejaculatory prayer, because it is so associated with a certain day and hour in August of a certain year in the critical period of his youth, when, walking in his father's garden, he gave his heart to Christ.

That wounded soldier who rebuked the winking stars on the field of Shiloh bethought him of a hymn which he used to sing when a boy in the Sunday school. Something moved him to sing it again; and he broke out with, —

> "When I can read my title clear
> To mansions in the skies," &c.

When the third line was reached, another voice joined his, then another and another; and when he began the second stanza, more than three hundred of those wounded men, some of them with faltering and dying accents, and again the gray and the blue together, wafted that Christian song over that field of blood.

Was there no prevision of a divine eye, no planning of a divine hand, in teaching them that hymn of holy triumph long years before? Was there no prompting of thoughtful and tender kindness in their being moved to sing it then when most they needed it? To many of them, doubtless, it was more than the wings of angels, bearing them up to the opening heavens.

We cannot convince a man of the reality of these awakening and creative influences in other lives, who has not felt them in his own. The power to see them is largely a matter of will. If I take a handful of steel-filings, and hold over them my ebony ruler, there is no motion. They lie still and dead. But if I take a magnet, that iron with a soul in it, and draw it slowly over them, every solitary particle springs in response, and clings to the electric metal as to a friend. So let a man whose faith in God is *wooden* review his own life, and he may find nothing suggestive to such faith. But once magnetize him with the will to see, and he cannot find so much as the space for a needle's point on which the love of God has not left its impress.

To eyes once opened to this truth, it throws a flood of golden light over the blackest and most tempestuous midnight of a troubled life. Such a man *knows* that there is a God in heaven whom the heaven of heavens cannot contain, but who deigns to dwell in the homes of men. You can neither prove it to him nor disprove it. He knows it. When scientists come bending under the weight of their learned volumes, proving beyond all question that God is not, he waves them off, smiling as at the bugaboo which scared his childhood in the dark.

4. The interlacing of the plans of God with the plans of men *goes far towards explaining the mystery of shocking and exceptional calamity.* Starting with the inexplicable *fact* of sin, there is little mystery left in any kind or degree. or combinations of *suffering*. In a world overrun with sin and steeped in guilt as this world is, suffering is no

mystery. It is God's great remedial antidote to sin. The mystery would be fearful if there were none. Suffering is a wonderful fertilizer to the roots of character. The great object of this life is character. This is the only thing we can carry with us into eternity. Benevolent discipline, therefore, is aimed at the accumulating, the consolidating, and the purifying, of character. To gain the most of it, and the best of it, is the object of probation.

For such an object, suffering must often take on a surgical severity. The right hand must be cut off, and the right eye plucked out. Who can say what suffering may not have done for that wretched prince of Judah in the dungeons of Chaldæa? The butchery of his children may have been the only thing that could drive him back to the God of his fathers. Blinded eyes and chained limbs may have been necessary to fit him for heaven. Those dark days and silent nights, — at a distance of twenty-five hundred years one shivers at the thought of them, — yet they may have been a grand opportunity for the Spirit of God to work in. God may have been waiting for it for fifty years. The doomed sufferer, but the saved sinner, may now be praising God for them. It will probably be one of the surprises of heaven, that we shall find there so many saved by God's loving use of last days, it may be of last hours, of speechless suffering here.

But what of the suffering of innocence and the awful inequalities of it in this world? What of those helpless, butchered little children of the Judæan king? Well, we admit that it is a tough question; yet it is not wholly unanswerable. The mystery is lightened when we take in God's conception of the evil of sin. Nothing can be too shocking to express divine abhorrence of that. The more startling and mysterious that expression, the more natural it is. Sin itself is the great anomaly of the universe. God's treatment of it should seem to be full of anomalies, strange and fearful. That is just what sin calls for. Hence the suffering of the innocent with and for the guilty. Yet, to the innocent, suffering is not vengeance; it is not punishment even: it is only the *discipline* which love chooses for their holy development. To them it is just what they are *conscious* of receiving. If conscious of no sin, they are conscious of no punishment.

Have you never seen the look of *age* on the countenance of an infant in its coffin? Suffering may have done rapidly the work of years of ordinary life there in creating character. That infant's chief praise in heaven may be for the fact that its brief life here was one of anguish. That may have been the chief instrument by which God has lifted it above the rank of a humming-bird.

Even when death in shocking and violent fury seems to overtake men unprepared, who shall say that infinite love, and love to *them*, may not have so ordained it? Men who have entered the valley of the shadow by drowning, and have come back to life, tell us of a strange quickening of the soul's capacities in those moments of suspended vitality. Souls live fast in last moments. Who can say, then, that the Spirit of God does not avail himself of that law of mind, and work fast in such moments? At the last trump, we shall be changed in the twinkling of an eye. Why not as well in the death-gasp? Oh! you and I must become a great deal wiser than we are now, in the hidden things of wisdom, before we can venture to raise a question even of the tenderness of God, in the most appalling tragedy which cold stars ever winked at, or merry bluebirds ever sang to in the hazel-bush.

5. The interworking of the plans of God with the plans of men *suggests the only true method of happy as well as holy living.* It is to make our plans one with God's plans. Thus blessedness is sure for both worlds. Study God's plans; study his providences; study his word; hearken for the whispers of his Spirit. Make much of still hours. Find out thus your place in God's purposes of procedure. Then drop into that place trustfully and contentedly. Move with his moves, start at his bidding, go here, go there, stay, as he directs. Lie still and suffer, if that be the order from above. Have no will but his. Pray no unquali-

fied prayers, except where he has revealed his will. Never plan without taking God into confidence, and asking him what he thinks of it. Never contend with God in secret feeling. Give way to no silent longings of discontent. Indulge no reveries over impossible blessings. When prayer has lifted you into harmony with him, do not fritter it away by repining after-thoughts. Never look backward: remember Lot's wife. Our chief miseries come from spiritual retrogrades. In short, be at one with God: so shall your peace flow like a river, and your joy shall be like the swellings of Jordan.

THE KINGDOMS THAT DIE, AND THE KINGDOM THAT LIVES.

> And in the days of these kings shall the God of heaven set up a kingdom which shall never be destroyed ; and the kingdom shall not be left to other people, but it shall break in pieces and consume all these kingdoms, and it shall stand forever. Forasmuch as thou sawest that the stone was cut out of the mountain without hands, and that it brake in pieces the iron, the brass, the clay, the silver, and the gold; the great God hath made known to the king what shall come to pass hereafter: and the dream is certain, and the interpretation thereof sure. — DAN. ii. 44, 45.

THIS enigmatical passage in the life of the Babylonian monarch is aptly summed up in the foregoing title. I must leave to the commentaries the disputed interpretation of this symbolic language, and confine my thought to the obvious principle involved in it, which extends over a broader area. It expresses a fragment of that universal law by which every thing human is doomed to decay, but to which there is one, and but one, mysterious exception.

1. The *law of decay in human affairs:* let us endeavor to obtain some fresh conception of it, as a law under which every human life passes.

(1) It is impressively illustrated in the fact *that individuals pass so soon out of the memory of the*

world. Individuals soon die, and the dead are soon forgotten. When a man dies, another man arises who will fill his place, and, as a rule, fill it as well as he has done. His business, his houses, his lands, his honors, his titles, will pass into other hands, and by the world at large he will not be missed. He will die out of the world's thought as thoroughly as his mouldering body passes out from the home which he once cheered, and from the seat at the table of which he was once the honored head.

A man's character may live. The influence he exerted may pass into other lives, but not in any such way as to identify his name, and keep that alive. That dies as surely as he dies, and not long after. Scientists tell us that it is a law of dynamics that a pin dropped to the surface of the earth sends a concussion through the universe. But who hears the falling pin? Who feels the force of the blow? What sleeper is awakened by it? Who identifies and remembers it? Similar is the law of individual influence. It lives, indeed, through all time, and penetrates eternity; but the man soon ceases to be known as its author. His decaying brain is not more securely buried in the grave from the sight of men, than his name is, sooner or later, from their memory. Such is the common course of human life. So it has been; so it is; so it must be; so it will be forever.

(2) This law of decay is more impressively illus-

trated *in the fact that nations die.* Why should not a proud and gallant nation, which *has* made a thousand years of history, make ten thousand more, — yes, live on forever? The monarch of the East was not without some reason for his boast, "Is not this great Babylon, which I have built?" Who shall dare to predict its downfall? It surely, with its walls three hundred and fifty feet high, and so broad that four chariots could drive abreast on their summit, — it surely had the *look* of eternity. "The Eternal City," the Romans proudly called their peerless capital, — and why not?

Yet what *is* the history of great empires? What but the record of the death-scenes of nations? The glory of one is the doom of another; the rise of one, the fall of its predecessor. So uniform has the process been, that philosophic historians have believed that the history of nations is foredoomed to run in a circle, not in a line. Rise, growth, glory, decay, fall, death, seem to tell the whole story. History seems like one vast obituary.

So complete is the oblivion which creeps over great nations, that in some cases the fact of their having lived is known only by melancholy inference from the fact that they have died. Antiquarians find in the East enormous burial-places, with cypresses overgrowing thousands of graves, when every other trace of the cities which once supplied them with their silent population has disappeared. The aboriginal mounds found in some parts of our own continent tell a similar story. Great nations doubtless once lived here, of which those burial-mounds are the only monument now extant. Not a page of written history, not a hieroglyph, remains to tell us who and what they were: their very names are blotted from the knowledge of mankind forever.

(3) This law of decay is illustrated instructively in the fact *that it disappoints the most plausible plans and expectations of men.* Endless are the expedients by which men struggle against death in the memory of their successors. Some have built pyramids; others have fought battles; others have written books or made discoveries; others have founded cities, libraries, schools, churches; others have established families among a hereditary nobility. How much of wasted mind has been expended on the science of heraldry! Yet not one of these lifelong struggles has succeeded in giving to any man the object of his ambition. The world forgot, more than a thousand years ago, who built some of the pyramids of Egypt. Long before that, men had ceased to care who founded Thebes or Palmyra. The impressiveness of such oblivion sometimes borders on the ludicrous. A few years ago I wandered over the ruins of old Rome, and what think you I saw among the ruins of the fallen palace of the Cæsars? A garden of cabbages! The vilest of vegetables had more power to perpetuate its kind than he whom men once wor-

shipped as a god, and of whom they said that a new star appeared in the heavens when he died. The only living successor of Nero and Caligula was a plain Mr. Smith, who had erected on those ruins a red-brick house, not more imposing than the one in which his namesake lives in Tenth Street, Philadelphia, or in Houston Street, New York.

Napoleon lamented that his conquests did not last as long as the time he occupied in making them. His own prediction was, that the time would come when all that the world would care to know of him would be comprised in half a page of history; and he was right. Sir Walter Scott fell into idiocy in his almost superhuman effort to place himself at the head of one of the noble families of Great Britain. But no child of his lives to inherit his honors or perpetuate his fame. *That* means of keeping alive the name of Walter Scott has failed forever.

The point I would emphasize by these illustrations is the fact that the law of decay which is written on all things human is so imperious in its sway that the most ingenious and stupendous exertions of men to achieve what they call immortality are overreached and defeated by it, and that therefore disappointment is written on thousands of wasted lives. The most long-lived of those whom the world calls immortal on the rolls of fame must at last accept the epitaph which the poet Keats suggested for his own: "Here lies one whose name was writ in water."

2. But to this law of decay in human affairs *there is one grand and marvellous exception.* God has a kingdom in this world, which lives.

(1) It deserves mention in illustration of this exception, that *the work of God in redemption is the only thing in human history that dates back to the beginning of time.* God's work in this world is the only thing now living that goes back into antediluvian history. It is the only thing which links the whole of human history together. Other things fall, die, rot, by the side of this: this lives on to the world's end.

The vanity of individuals, the ambition of families, the pride of cities, the glory of nations, the conflicts of races, — all have been short-lived. But it has not been so with this work of God. Fortunes are dissipated in a tithe of the time which it requires to amass them. Commercial panics prostrate merchant princes in an hour. Treasures are sunk in the sea or in storms of fire. The very highways of *commerce* are changed by events which no human foresight can provide for. Cities like Venice and the Hanse towns, once the centres of great trades, are left like stranded ships, and the commerce of the world flows elsewhere. Kingdoms, too, perish from the memory of men. Races become extinct. But it is not so with this work of God.

The very *sciences* of the world fluctuate. The knowledge of one age becomes folly to the next. The universities of to-day laugh at those of yesterday. Culture runs the gauntlet of system after system of philosophy, of political economy, of art, which seem to have been created only for the sake of dying. Pursuits once dignified as sciences, such as astrology, alchemy, magic, are exploded. But it is not so with this work of God.

The world's *religions*, too, have succumbed to the same law of doom. A religious system once rooted in the civilization of a people is the last thing to die. But many such have expired. Others are in the process of dissolution. Even the *languages* in which men transmit their treasures of learning, civilization, and religion, die. What an appalling thing to the imagination is a dead language! Every thing that man originates lives but a brief time in a world's life. But it is not so with this work of God.

Amidst disorganizing forces that shake to pieces every thing else, this work lives, with the fixedness of the North Star. Other things bend to this: this never yields to them. All force in this world, sooner or later, yields to this unarmed and silent power. In every thing else the iron and the brass and the clay become like the chaff of the summer threshing-floor; while the stone cut out without hands is growing to a great mountain, and filling the whole earth.

(2) The contrast between the kingdoms of men and the kingdom of God is further seen in *the mysterious vitality of right in this world, in its conflicts with wrong.* Evil, organized never so deftly, becomes effete. Good seems robust and always growing. The right, in the outset of a great conflict with wrong, is always underneath; yet it always comes uppermost. It is never safe to an evil thing to agitate it. Inquiry is death to it. In every conflict the right gains something. It never loses a battle. Its drawn battles are secret victories. When Edmund Burke said to the first military and naval power of the world, "You *cannot* conquer America," he spoke a principle which runs through all historic struggle of wrong with right.

It is astonishing what heroic deeds men who are not above their fellows in strength of religious principle will dare to undertake, if sustained by a consciousness of being in the right. Why are a dozen policemen, on the side of law, a match for a hundred desperadoes in a riot? When the Continental Congress was debating the question of independence of the mother-country, more than half the world believed it would never dare to do the deed. English statesmen smiled incredulously when it was threatened. When the "Declaration" was under discussion, and it was rumored that it would be signed that day, an old man was sent into the belfry of Independence Hall, in

Philadelphia, where the Congress was in session, and directed to strike one hundred strokes on "Liberty Bell" when the act was done. The old man sauntered up the spiral stairs muttering, "They will never do it; they will never do it." He spoke the feeling of more than half his contemporaries the world over. The hours went slowly by: the old man fell asleep at his post, but was at length roused by a shout from "State House yard:" "Ring, ring! they've done it!" And the hundred tongues of "Liberty Bell" told the world that fifty-five[1] men had defied the first naval power of Europe.

They had done it at the risk of their lives. Every man who signed that scroll committed high treason. When the last name was written, a silence fell upon the assembly, in which every man thought of the scaffold. So oppressive was the stillness, that Franklin felt the need of lifting the mood of his colleagues to one more cheerful; and he uttered the *bon mot* which has since become famous: "Now we must all hang together, or we shall all *hang* separately."

Nothing could have sustained such men in such a deed but the simple consciousness that they were *in the right*. Among them were praying men, whose thought was of the God of battles.

---

[1] Common history says "fifty-six." But one of the number was absent at the time, and was permitted to add his name some time after.

The clause near the end of the Declaration, "With a firm reliance on Divine Providence," was not in the original draft by Jefferson. It was inserted as an amendment by unanimous vote. That appeal to God, in behalf of right, was more to them than the fleets of England, which whitened all the harbors of the world. Right in the affairs of men is the synonyme of God. It lives because he lives. It is eternal because he is eternal.

3. The contrast between God's kingdom and the kingdoms of this world is further seen *in an anomalous suspension of the law of decay in some cases of historic immortality.* The only men who are destined to live while the world lives are those who are in some way especially identified with the kingdom of Christ. The only nations which will escape the decline and fall which have thus far made up the dismal round of history are those which shall be given to Christ, and shall realize the Christian ideal of national life in the civilization of the future. The perpetuity of the Hebrew nation is the great miracle of history, unparalleled by the fate of any other people on the globe under similar conditions. They live because they were once, and are to be again, the chosen people of God in executing the purposes of redemption.

Such exceptions are perceptible even in the experience of individuals. Compare a good man and a bad man in any community, in respect to the memory of them which lives after them. The good man always lives longer, in the memory of survivors, than the bad man of the same amount of character, and with equal conditions of power. Never did inspiration utter a truer apothegm than in recording that " the memory of the wicked shall *rot.*"

4. Here belongs the fact that the only names from the remote past which in the nature of things *can* go down to the world's latest ages, *are those which are to be immortalized by the Christian Scriptures.*

This book is the only literature of the *first* times which *can* live in the vivid and fresh interest of men to the *last* times.

It is a pleasant thought, that the very names which we revere in the biblical biographies will seem to the last generations of the race to be the only immortal names in history. The very stories which we teach to our children from these inspired pages will fascinate the children and the children's children of the world's closing ages. Abel, Abraham, Joseph, David, Isaiah, Daniel, John the Baptist, St. Paul, the Virgin Mary, will live in the reverence of the remotest times, when not a guess at their existence could survive the ravages of time but for the place they hold in the execution of God's work and in the record of it in God's word.

The eleventh chapter of the Epistle to the Hebrews will immortalize certain names, which now are not known to half the world. That poor woman who broke the box of alabaster on the person of her Lord is to have a memorial of that act preserved for her among all nations and through all time. She will be the subject of study to Christian scholars when the Pyramids of Egypt shall have crumbled. What will the world care then for Cheops in comparison with this nameless woman? Her deed of love to Christ will give her a name above all the honors of heraldry. It is an affecting comment on the destiny of all things human, that the only thing which is to hand down the name of the *first* man of our race to the *last* man is that plan of God in the structure of the Bible which has wrought the name of Adam into the story of redemption.

A single reflection is suggested by this review. It is the glory of the Christian Church. Who can help exulting in it? In this Church of the living God is concentrated all that is eternal in this world's history. It is identified with God, and God is identified with it. Its work is God's work. Already its history laps over into another world. It has sent forward its advance-guard in innumerable hosts who are waiting for the rear-guard. But a little stream divides them. That stream itself is populous with the multitudes who are crossing over.

> "Just before, the shining shore
> We may almost discover."

It is a privilege — is it not? — to be a member of the Church of Christ; to constitute *one* of this mighty and immortal host; to bear the name which it bears; to unite in its songs, and be remembered in its prayers; to be identified with its work, and to share its rewards; to be counted worthy of its sufferings, and to earn the fruit of its heroism: what has life to offer to a good man of lofty aspirations which can bear comparison with this? I never think of a child of God outside of the Church of Christ, but with feelings of unutterable compassion. He is losing so much which might be his; he is failing to achieve so much which might swell his reward at the Master's coming!

He reminds me of the story of "The Man without a Country," doomed, in punishment of his momentary treason, never to hear from human lips the *name* of the land that gave him birth. He crossed oceans in his country's service, but could never hear her glory told. Her insignia were torn from the badge of his uniform. When his companions exulted over the news of her victories, dead silence stopped all voices if he entered their circle. The newspaper from home was not permitted to pass into his hands till it had been reviewed by a censor, and the name of his country expurgated from its columns. Though an honest sailor and a gallant officer, his name appeared nowhere on the roll of his country's fame. He lived and died a nameless man, without a country and without a home.

Such a one does a Christian seem, who is trying to serve God and make his way to heaven outside of and out of sympathy with the Church of Christ. What can be done with such a man in heaven? What regrets must mingle with his joys on entering there! "Do *this* in remembrance of me." That one command, given in the parting hour by the loving Saviour to loved disciples, he has never in his whole life obeyed.

Oh, thanks to God for his visible Church! for her hymns and her prayers, for her ordinances and the promises she inherits, for the fellowship of the saints on earth with saints in heaven, for the history of her sufferings, and the future of her triumphs! Thank God for her *immortality!* While every thing else in this world must die and rot, there is *one* thing that lives, one thing over which death has no power, one thing that smiles at the grave as it passes on to a life that has no end!

FRUITLESS CONVICTIONS OF SIN.

Belshazzar the king made a great feast to a thousand of his lords, and drank wine before the thousand. . . . In the same hour came forth fingers of a man's hand, and wrote over against the candlestick upon the plaster of the wall of the king's palace; and the king saw the part of the hand that wrote. Then the king's countenance was changed, and his thoughts troubled him, so that the joints of his loins were loosed, and his knees smote one against another. . . . And this is the writing that was written: MENE, MENE, TEKEL, UPHARSIN. This is the interpretation of the thing: MENE; God hath numbered thy kingdom, and finished it. TEKEL; Thou art weighed in the balances, and art found wanting. PERES; Thy kingdom is divided, and given to the Medes and Persians. . . . In that night was Belshazzar the king of the Chaldæans slain. — DAN. v. 1, 5, 6, 25-28, 30.

WASHINGTON ALLSTON spent more than twelve years attempting to paint the scene of Belshazzar's feast, and then left his work unfinished. It is said that the chief difficulty, which the artist's genius could not overcome, was that of depicting the despair of the doomed king. Well it might be so; for it was the despair of a lost soul brought suddenly face to face with the retributive judgment of God, written by a mysterious hand from another world. What art *can* portray it in the look of a human face?

This Chaldæan monarch is one of the few *indi-*

vidual cases mentioned in the Scriptures, of men whose damnation in eternity is made morally certain. Rarely, even in the case of a very wicked man, does the inspired writer lift the veil from individual destiny, and assure us that it is fatal. But in this instance there can scarcely be room for doubt. The implications of doom are overwhelming. Belshazzar had been long familiar with a knowledge of the true God. He had had miraculous evidences of it in the experience of his father. "Thou knewest all this," is the faithful reminder which the prophet gives him. Yet he had persisted in a life and reign of extreme and unblushing guilt. "O Belshazzar, thou hast not humbled thine heart; but hast lifted up thyself against the Lord of heaven." Then appeared the fearful writing on the wall, the purport of which is too plain to admit of doubt. That night the king was summoned to the bar of God.

This may be fairly assumed, therefore, as a case of *clear and prolonged conviction of sin which did not result in the soul's salvation.* Who of us has the heart to follow the doomed monarch beyond the scenes of that awful night? Let us draw the veil over that unwritten and unutterable future, and turn to a class of men whose experience on the subject of religion is not dissimilar, so far as this, — that they have long known the truth, have long felt themselves to be sinners before God, yet they stop just there, with the acknowledged sense of sin often lying as a wearisome weight on their souls, and never relieved by repentance and the consciousness of peace with God. If they were to be suddenly called into God's presence with hearts unchanged, as the Chaldæan king was, the verdict of the mysterious hand would be the same: "Thou art weighed in the balances, and art found wanting."

One young man I once knew, in whose mind these very words rested for months, as the summing up of his own character and destiny. "Weighed, and found wanting,"—the words were like a live coal upon his eyeballs. Wherever he looked he saw them. They glared upon him from the walls of his chamber. All faith, all hope, was buried in them. Outwardly he lived like other men. Few knew the dull nightmare of conscious and despairing guilt in which he lived. Yet rarely was he conscious of an hour when *he* did not feel it, resting like a pall over the joys of this world, and foreshadowing in silent prophecy his doom in another. He represented a class of men who are not few, who suffer for years under hopeless and fruitless convictions of sin.

There are certain truths which one who is living in the state of mind here described needs especially to consider.

1. One is that *the suffering which accompanies hopeless conviction of sin is no more than a sinner deserves.* Hopeless consciousness of sin is re-

morse; and remorse is the natural vengeance of sin upon a sinner. It is legitimate: it is just. We are never wronged in the vengeance of remorse. God has not wronged us in making us susceptible of such suffering; conscience does not wrong us in inflicting it; the holy universe does not wrong us in approving it.

We have no reason to compassionate ourselves as if we were only unfortunates in the gloom of hopeless guilt. That is an enervating state of mind in which a convicted sinner pities himself because he feels that he is a sufferer. Conviction must probe our souls deeper than that. We must condemn ourselves, and justify God, even if he should leave us in that furnace of burning remorse through eternity. Never a man of us will truly accept Christ as a Saviour, who does not so feel his own guilt as to drop the sense of injury, and justify God in his condemnation. "Eternal sin deserves eternal woe," — until we feel this in our inmost being, we have no adequate sense of what sin is, — no adequate sense, therefore, of our need of Christ; and we accept Christ never but as a necessity.

One man lived in such an overwhelming consciousness of ill-desert, that, when death approached, he wrote to a friend, "Let me beg of you, as you value your old friend, not to suffer any pomp to be used at my funeral, nor any monumental inscription to mark where I am laid.

Lay me quietly in the earth: place a sun-dial over my grave, and let me be forgotten." Yet that man was John Howard. The best of men feel most profoundly the conviction of ill-desert as a part of the conviction of sin. Until a sinner feels this, he cannot feel that Christ is a necessity to him; and there is no peace for him.

2. Yet one who suffers under unavailing convictions should see *that it is no proper effect of religion to produce such convictions.* On no subject do we confound causes and effects more egregiously than on this. We charge upon religion the misery which arises from the want of it. The legitimate tendency of piety in the soul is all benignant. The fruit of the Spirit — what is it? Love, joy, peace. Glad tidings of great joy, this is the gospel. It is a volume of benedictions.

Elementary truths are these; yet the sense of guilt often crowds them out of sight. A sinner feels the throes of remorse, and says within himself, "This is the fruit of religion." His former gayety he contrasts with his present misery; and he reflects, "This is what religion does for a man." The world looks upon the change in him, and says, "See the working of your religion: it is a sour-faced business!" Not so, not so. There is no religion in suffering as such. There is no religion in fear, in conviction of guilt, in self-reproach, in forebodings of hell. A prolonged endurance of these is no necessary preliminary to the peace of a forgiven soul. Some converted men have never experienced them in protracted or despairing agony.

Says Dr. Chalmers, "I cannot say of myself that I ever felt a state of mind corresponding to John Bunyan's 'Slough of Despond.' What am I to infer from this? That I have not yet surmounted the impassable barrier that stands between me and the gate of life? So one would suppose from John Bunyan. So I would suppose, myself, were it not for the assurance of the Saviour, 'He that believeth in me, though he were dead yet shall he live.' This is my firm hold, and I will not let it go."

No, there are no grooves in which the experience anterior to the joy of pardon must run long and gloomily, as through an unlighted tunnel. The tumultuous conflicts which some endure, at a certain crisis of their religious history, are the conflicts of sin, — not *with* sin, but *of* sin. They are the sheer obstinacy of guilt resisting its own condemnation by the just mind of God. They are the death-struggle of sin, prolonged only so long as the sinner withholds himself from Christ. In the rapids of a cataract, the bare struggle to stand still may strain the muscles to agony. So, in the midst of convictions of guilt, and the strivings of the Holy Spirit, a sinner's sheer effort to remain a sinner may wrench all joy out of him.

3. A third truth which should command the

faith of one who endures ineffectual convictions of sin is, *that God is a sinner's friend.* It seems irreverent to affirm this, as if a doubt of it were conceivable. Yet towards no other one truth is the human heart so faithless. The instinct of sin is to look upon God as not only the enemy of sin, but the enemy of the sinner as well.

Under Christian light, right here beneath the meridian of Christian illumination, men do not know God as their friend. "*May* I love God?" was the trembling and faithless query of one penitent believer. When sin dawns upon the sinner's conscience as a reality, it starts up the thought of God as an enemy. We are apt to count that man our enemy to whom we are enemies. Nature says, "He will injure me, whom I have injured." Sin is twin brother to Hate.

Said an injured man at the capital of our country, justifying himself for taking the life of his enemy, "He wronged me in that one thing in which no man ever forgives his fellow. He and I cannot live on the same globe together." So it is human nature to reason about God. "He is my enemy because I am his." The world seems to be losing its youth, and growing old before its time, in the struggle of the ages to rid itself of this *satanic* conception of God. That there is one Being in the universe, who, with no taint in his ineffable purity, can look down upon this world with mild, pitying, forgiving eyes, — this one

FRUITLESS CONVICTIONS OF SIN. 251

thought of God in Christ is the conception of him against which guilt has been contending for six thousand years.

One who suffers under prolonged and abortive convictions of sin should therefore admit this faith to his heart, — that God is a sinner's friend. Not merely that Christ is his friend. A strange and murky distortion sometimes gets possession of us. It is that somehow God and Christ are not at one in friendliness to the guilty. The idea does not define itself sharply. If it did, a man's good sense would reject it. But, if defined, it would be something like this, — that, while Christ desires to save men, back of his atoning work there stands a frowning and relentless Deity, who is averse to the whole procedure by which a sinner escapes eternal woe. God, as such, is eager to damn a sinner. The necessities of his holy nature are such that he enjoys the outpouring of his wrath in eternal fires. God, as such, therefore, is the sinner's enemy. In the blackness of darkness which overwhelms a despairing soul, these two conceptions of God as love, and God as a consuming fire, often wrestle like masked combatants.

In the final extreme, there comes about that state of guilty conviction without hope which one of the most earnest thinkers of England described by saying, "Life, the world, mankind, religion, eternity, all appear to me like one vast scene of confusion, stretching away before me, and closed in shades of the most dreadful darkness, — a darkness which only the most powerful splendors of Deity can illumine, and which appears as if *they never had illumined it.*"

I have somewhere read a story of a man who was locked into a darkened chamber at midnight and alone, with a maniac in a paroxysm of silent and cunning bloodthirst. Crouching in one corner, the horror-struck man could hear the creaking of the floor under the cat-like tread of the demoniac as he crept after him. He moved noiselessly to another corner; but soon he felt the magnetic sense of the proximity of the foe he could not see and dared not touch. Springing past him in the darkness, he could perceive the taint of his hot breath, and could hear his quick panting, and the grinding of his teeth in disappointed rage. Moments were ages in the waiting for the death-grapple. When the morning dawned, and relief came, and the windows were thrown open, his raven hair was turned snow-white.

To such insane companionship does hopeless guilt doom a man at the last in the communings of his soul with God. With trembling reverence be it said, if God were an Almighty Maniac he could scarcely be an object of more profound terror or more relentless hate. This is no fiction. Some heathen tribes have worshipped just such a god. It is a frightful confirmation of the biblical conception of sin, that when the human mind loses all knowledge of the true God, the Devil takes his place. And not the Devil in lofty and aspiring malignity like that of Milton's Satan, but in grovelling or insane distortions which the soul shudders at, yet yields to. "Fall down and worship me," is the dread command; and it is obeyed. Demoniac idols in heathen temples bear a frightful resemblance to the faces of maniacs.

Now, so long as such a nightmare of horror as this broods over a man, think you that he can have peace?

The power which conquers guilt is the omnipotence of love. Let it be repeated and reiterated therefore, — God is the sinner's friend. Throw open the windows to the light of heaven. Let the glory of God stream in from golden skies! The *whole* Godhead is the sinner's friend. "I will rejoice to do them good with my *whole* heart and with my *whole* soul." There is no Nemesis crouching with malign cunning behind the cross. God is never more the sinner's friend than in the very quickening of conscience which he resists.

It has been said, that, in such a world as this, "a man may have too much love to weep." So in the appalling extremity to which sin has reduced mankind, God has too much love to beguile them with a maudlin kindness which would not pain them by a disclosure of their guilt to their own souls. God is intent on their salvation, not so much from suffering as from sin. Sin is the maelstrom which sucks into its vortex all joy, all peace, all hope. God strains the resources of his wisdom and his power to rescue men from eternal guilt. He condescends to enter into conflict with them to save them from themselves. Such is his faithful, his enduring, his long-suffering, his overwhelming friendship. His indeed is love which many waters cannot quench, nor floods drown. George Fox describes his own discovery of this truth, in language which portrays the experience of all who are enlightened by the grace of God. He says, "I saw that there was an ocean of darkness and death. But an infinite ocean of light and love flowed *over* the ocean of darkness; and in *that* I saw the infinite love of God."

At some point in our mental history, if we are ever to be saved, we must let into our souls that mighty and swelling flood of benignity which God has poured forth in this work for our deliverance from guilt, and in which the whole heart of the Godhead has been expressed. Said one, reflecting upon the disclosures of God in nature, "Flowers surely are smiles of God's goodness." — "Yes," said his friend with a deeper insight, "yes; but the fairest flower I ever saw climbing around a poor man's window was never so beautiful in my eyes as the Bible which I saw lying within." So should we look at the goodness of God, as it is seen in the revelation of the brightness of the

Father's glory. Nowhere else do we feel as we do here, that God is a sinner's friend.

4. Again, one who labors under fruitless convictions needs to see that *the chief obstacle to his salvation is not the want of a more perfect understanding of the theory of conversion.* This suggests a peculiar delusion under which men often suffer, when convinced of sin without repentance. We are apt to fancy, in such a state, that we should be saved more easily if we understood the process more philosophically. *Our* work would be more practicable if we could see into *God's* work more cunningly.

If we could lift the curtain that hides the decrees of God; if we could discover how prayer can affect the decree concerning our salvation, which was fixed before we had souls to save; if we could solve the riddle of impenitent prayer; if we could satisfy reason as to the responsibility of a sinner whose heart God has hardened in some sense, as he did Pharaoh's; in brief, if the tangled knot of the divine and the human in one, which is laced most inseparably in the doctrine of conversion, could be untwisted, and its filaments straightened out side by side, — we cannot resist the feeling that we should breathe more freely, and look heavenward more hopefully.

The point I would emphasize, therefore, is that the chief obstruction to a man's salvation never lies in any such difficulty as that. A sinner needs to admit this and to feel it. It may be that even a legitimate interest in the theory of religion — that is, an interest right enough in itself, and at some time and for some minds important — is not timely to your mind now and here. Some minds need, for their healthy and practical working in religious matters, a reduction of speculative tone. Religious speculation often reaches a condition like that which medical science calls "sub-acute inflammation." It needs to be reduced to less feverish inquiry.

The Rev. John Foster of Bristol was probably by nature one of the most sceptical men who have ever been led to accept Christ as a Saviour. It was a long stride towards the salvation of such a soul as his when he was led to say, as he did at last, after long despair, "I have felt the necessity of dismissing subtle speculations, and of yielding a humble, cordial assent to mysterious truth, just *as* and *because* the Scriptures declare it, without asking, 'How can these things be?' The gospel is to me a matter of urgent *necessity*. I come to Jesus because I *need* pardon." So must every sinner come, — not beguiled by the solution of difficulties, but driven by a sense of necessities. The vast majority of us never come in any other way.

5. The chief obstacle to the termination of fruitless convictions in peace with God is to be found *in some plain, practical affair of character and real*

life. No feeling, I think, is more common among those who have found peace in Christ, after protracted and remorseful conflict, than the feeling of *surprise* that they have been kept aloof from Christ so long. They have been looking up into the clouds, struggling with aching eyes to see visions; or have introverted their thoughts upon themselves, straining to see their own eyeballs: while the real obstacle to their conversion has been in plain sight at their feet, — a little thing perhaps; a trifling thing, as they now regard it; in comparison with Christ, a contemptible thing. They are humiliated at the discovery that so mean a thing has had power to hold them back from the wide-open gates of heaven. It seems to them, in the retrospect, like some invisible and malignant magic in the air.

I have seen a diseased man fascinated by a piece of magnetized iron not so large as my hand. He would gaze upon it as if, like a serpent, it had charmed him. He would follow it from room to room, in agony lest it should pass out of his sight. He would chase it in the street, and lie down and grovel in the dust where it was thrown. He seemed as if his spirit had in part passed out of him, and had entered that magnet.

Thus demented do converted men sometimes seem to themselves to have been, when they look back over the unseen line which separates them from their impenitent life, and see what a paltry thing it was which held them so long transfixed in those fruitless convictions, while a crucified Saviour was pleading with them and dying for them, within reach of their hand. Such has been the experience of thousands, and doubtless will be of thousands more.

The charms by which the sorcery of sin thus bewitches men are very numerous, and diverse in character. In one man it is a distrust of God's willingness to save, or, if to save, to save *him*. In another, it is an unwillingness to own the simplicity of God's methods of salvation. In another it is a desire for a gorgeous experience, like that of exceptional Christian memoirs. In the vast majority, however, it is not in any conceptions cherished about the way of salvation, but in something altogether more tangible and earthly. The whole truth is, that the man *loves something more than God*. In one it is his property; in another, his reputation; in another, his ease; in another, his literary tastes; in another, an unchristian employment or habit or association, which he feels to be at war with an earnest Christian life. He foresees, that, if he becomes a Christian, that must be given up. In some it is an unwillingness publicly to profess religion, to perform certain public or social religious duties, to encounter the ridicule of companions, or to forgive an injury which rankles in the heart.

Some such very simple thing is the citadel in

FRUITLESS CONVICTIONS OF SIN. 259

which the forces of guilty resolve intrench themselves. That is the secret reason why the soul is benighted in impotent convictions. Yet what a meanness of spirit does it seem to have indicated when the soul comes out into the liberty of Christ, to have shut itself up in that prison-house of remorse so long, and for such a thing!

I have somewhere read of an obscure Scotch woman whom Dr. Chalmers, as the story ran, was once summoned at midnight to attend in her last hours. She had lived for many years in sterile conviction of her sinfulness. Her anguish at last threatened her reason. "Weighed in the balances, and found wanting!" This was the burden she was carrying into eternity. With that kindly sympathy and tact for which Chalmers was noted in his ministrations to the ignorant, he sat down by her side, heard the story of her life, now and then aiding her to state her own case, for he knew it better than she did; and at length, when she had been calmed by the expression of her burden, he pointed out to her the one simple thing which he conjectured to have been *the* thing that had withheld her from Christ. The profoundest doctrine of our theology he told her as a simple story in her own Lowland dialect, and then told her, in the same rude speech of her childhood, that she must *give up that thing* for Christ's sake. The heavy-laden one, who had borne her infirmity for many years, and could in no wise lift up herself, looked up and said, but half believing, "And is that a'?" It was as if the Lord himself had laid his hand upon her. Immediately she was made straight, and glorified God.

So, many a penitent believer at the last recalls his bondage in sin, and exclaims, "Is that all that kept me so long away from Christ?"

THE MEN IN THE FIRE.

Shadrach, Meshach, and Abednego answered and said to the king, O Nebuchadnezzar, we are not careful to answer thee in this matter. If it be so, our God whom we serve is able to deliver us from the burning fiery furnace, and he will deliver us out of thy hand, O king. But if not, be it known unto thee, O king, that we will not serve thy gods, nor worship the golden image which thou hast set up. — DAN. iii. 16-18.

FEW men have the fortitude to bear the application of the moxa. When Senator Sumner was once inquired of, whether he found it intolerable, he evaded the query, saying, "Well, fire is fire. I believe the world has no two opinions about that." When St. Paul would express the severity of the trial of the eternal judgment, to which every man's work in life is to be subjected, he terms it "the trial as by fire."

Yes, fire is fire. Men in a furnace at white heat are not blamable, as the world judges, if they fling religious scruples to the winds. If wise men grow mad, if calm men become furious, if honest men are false, if devout men swear, the world finds no heart to rebuke them; for are they not men in the fire?

Not so thought and reasoned and acted the

three youthful victims of Chaldæan vengeance. They stand at the head of the long line of martyrs by fire in Christian history. Thousands in later times, some even younger than they, have walked calmly to the stake, cheered by the words of these young Hebrew exiles. Their great service to the world of subsequent ages is their teaching by word and act *the nature and the working of a religion of principle.*

1. They illustrate the truth that a religion of principle is *founded on intelligent convictions of truth, so fixed in the heart as to be beyond the reach of argument.* Their answer to the king's command has been the watchword of martyrs from that day to this: "We are not careful to answer thee in this matter. . . . But be it known unto thee, O king, that we will not serve thy gods."

There is a state of religious experience, possible to every Christian, of which this is a sample. It is a state in which the believer no longer needs argument to support his convictions, and is no longer open to argument against them. Certain central truths of religion are fixed in his very soul. They have been settled once for all and forever. An oak of a hundred years' growth is not rooted so immovably. They are thus settled, because they have become matters of *experience.* They long ago passed out of the realm of theory into the realm which Whitefield called "soul-life." The believer no longer believes: he knows. His faith has become his life. It has passed into the same rank of truths as that of gravitation. It gives to the whole religious being of the man a certain planetary fixedness and serenity, like those of Orion and the Pleiades. Canst thou *loose* the bands of Orion?

On such foundations a religion of principle is built. When infidelity assails it, when ridicule scoffs at it, when science disproves it, when authority forbids it, when fire and sword and gibbet would crush it, its calm reply is, "We are not careful to answer thee, but we will *not*." In these very words the father of the Wesleys sent back his answer to an iniquitous order from James II. of England.

When Philip II. of Spain sent "Alva the Butcher" on his crusade against the people of the Netherlands, thousands of men, women, and children sent back from the scaffold and the stake these words of calm defiance: "We are not careful to answer, but be it known that we will not obey." Children from ten to fifteen years of age used to imitate in solemn sport the scene of the *auto-da-fé*, in token of their resolve to die in the faith of their fathers. And when the sport became grim reality, and their tender limbs shrivelled and crackled in the flames, they did not flinch. That was the religion of principle, uttering itself from the depths of a "soul-life," which had outlived the need of argument to support it, and the power of argument to change it.

What could those children know of the argument for Christian truth, which ages of debate and of august councils had elaborated? They neither knew, nor cared to know. They had received from God a profounder teaching. Theirs was an experience of truth in the soul's life. They knew it because they had *lived* it. They could as easily have been argued out of their faith in the sunrise, as out of their faith in Christ. Just that kind of evidence and that degree of conviction are the privilege of every child of God.

2. The religion of principle consists pre-eminently *in obedience to the sense of duty, without regard to consequences.* So far as it appears from the story of these "men in the fire," this was their reasoning, and the whole of it: "We have only to do *right*, in the fear of God." Not a word is uttered from which we can infer that they think for one moment of what is or is not expedient. They are in a strait in which they may well be pardoned if they do ask themselves: "Can we not somehow save our lives?" Not a word of that sort appears, except a sublime assurance that God will save them, but a more sublime purpose to obey him whether he will or not. No nice points occur to them to be settled; no possible evasions; no concealment of their convictions; no hiding of their purposes.

Volumes have been written by wise men on questions relating to possible escape from martyrdom by crafty victims. "May a man lie to save his life from the flames? Has an enemy to God a right to know the truth from one to whom a disclosure of the truth is death? How much of one's faith may one hold in secret, under threat of axe and gibbet? For wife and children may not a man lie, when he would not to save his own life?" Said one, "I will not tell one falsehood to save my life, but I will tell ten to save my boy." Not a hint of any such Jesuitical strategy do these victims of pagan ferocity give us. There is a magnificent *fling* of self-abandonment in their sole resolve and its bold avowal, "Be it *known* that we will *not*." Moreover, the grandeur of the whole procedure is that their conscience is so eagle-eyed as to *see* the right on the spur of the moment. They are not startled into a momentary equivocation. When good men deny Christ, they are commonly surprised into it. Not so these three captives of the fire. They might be the three "wise men of the East," for their self-collected and clear-headed discernment of the right. With the hell of the furnace in the one scale, and beautiful young life in the other, there is not an instant of doubt which shall kick the beam. Said a Roman general, when urged to save his life at the cost of his honor, "It is necessary that my honor should live: it is not necessary that I should." So say these gentle youth, as they look into the mouth of that white furnace: "It is necessary that we be true to God: it is not necessary that we live."

Always is it characteristic of a religion of principle, that it gives small place to questions of expediency, except where the right depends on the expedient. The strength of godly principle is proportioned to its godly simplicity. It works with a noble independence of complicated motives and the intricacies of diplomacy. It never *undermines* a duty by questions of casuistry. Twists and doublings of conscience are not to its taste. Straight on it moves, to life if it may, to death if it must. This gives to such a type of religious character a marvellous power when confronted with this world of stratagem and duplicity.

The old mythology tells a story of a labyrinth of three thousand chambers, so contrived that no man had ever come out of it alive. The victim doomed to explore its dark recesses wandered on in hopeless mazes, turning this way and that, doubling on his track, confused by his own footsteps, dismayed by the sound of the bones of previous victims as he trampled on them, till at last, worn out with weariness and hunger and thirst and fright, he laid himself down, friendless and alone, to die. At length one prisoner bethought himself of the simple expedient of a ball of silk, the filament of which was scarcely visible to the eye. One end of it he fastened at the entrance, and then unrolled it as he advanced. Thus he explored the cave of doom, from whence no mortal had returned to the light of day before.

When he had reached its remotest chambers he had only to wind up again the silken thread, and follow it back to light and life. Such a filament of silken simplicity is duty, to one who is sent into the intricacies and snares of this world on probation for eternity.

3. The religion of principle *carries with it a profound sense of a personal God.* " Our *God* whom we serve." This is the first and last and ruling thought of these youthful heroes. Duty is no abstraction to them. They are not philosophers. They are simply believers in a living God. Poor souls! they know no better. They have never heard of the " Over-Soul " and the "Soul of the world." They have not been taught the dignity of their descent from baboons, by the force of "natural selection." Advanced thinkers have not instructed them in the religion of "protoplasm." But they do the best they know, humbly hoping that things will not go hard with them for trusting in a personal God. They enter into no discussion of the Hebrew as compared with the Chaldæan ethics. God, the living God, is the beginning and the end of the whole business.

A singular type of religious belief — or negation, call it which you please — has sprung up in our day, perhaps for the first time in the world's history. It proposes to build a system of Christian ethics on the intuitions of conscience alone, denying the authority of Christ and the being of a God. "Do right," is its moral law. "Obey conscience." "Care not for Jesus of Nazareth: he was a man like the rest of us. As for God, have no fear of him: he is a bugaboo of dark ages."

Never was a more unnatural monstrosity manufactured as the basis of a practical religion for men in their right minds. The Tartar who made his windmill do his praying for him, and the Frenchman who politely left his card on the cathedral altar, had not a more ignoble notion of religion. A healthy mind recoils from it as an absurdity.

To such a mind, duty and God are correlative ideas. Each is inseparable from the other. The force of each corresponds to the force of the other in the faith of the believer. Talk to a man of duty, and his instinctive query is, "Duty to whom?" Tell a man that he *ought*, and he rejoins, "Ought? why?" "Ought" implies obligation: obligation to whom? The very structure of the language mirrors a *person*. It means that or nothing. This mysterious indweller which we call "conscience," and which is the still guest of every man, is simply God writing his will on the walls of the soul's inner chambers. It is imperative as God is, pure as God is, deathless as God is. To hold to conscience, and deny God, is to grasp the shadow, and reject the substance.

The New England Pilgrims have been lauded

for the strength of their religious principle in not landing on the coast of Plymouth on the Lord's Day. Sixty-six days they had spent in a ship of but a hundred and eighty tons' burden. Some were prostrate with disease. The ship had sprung a leak. It would have been a great comfort to them to have set foot once more on solid land. But the day was holy time. They would not do violence to their consciences by needless labor. They waited in the close and comfortless cabin till the sabbath's sun went down. The world has rung with their praises from that day to this, for that act of sacrifice to a principle of conscience.

But how did those devotees of conscience spend those hours of holy time? Did they engage in mystic converse on the dignity of man, the supremacy of conscience, the godhead of self? Did they commune with each other upon the sublimity of law without a lawgiver; of conscience without a God; of Christianity without a Christ? Did they amuse themselves with any such religious cat's-cradle, experimenting to see how many senseless and useless curiosities in ethics they could make out of it? Not they. They lifted up their voices over that frozen coast in songs of praise and prayer to the living One. I seem to hear them singing, in commemoration of their deliverance from the perils of the sea, the old quaint version, by Sternhold and Hopkins, of the eighteenth Psalm: —

> "The Lord descended from above,
>   And bowed the heavens hie;
> And underneath his feete he cast
>   The darknesse of the skie.
>
> On cherubs and on cherubins
>   Full royallie he rode;
> And on the winges of all the windes,
>   Came flying alle abroad.
>
> And from above the Lord sent downe,
>   To fetch me from belowe;
> And pluckt me out of waters great,
>   That would me overflow.
>
> He brought me foorth in open place,
>   Whereas I might be free;
> And kept me safe because he had
>   A favour unto mee."

To them right living was living to God. Conscience was but the echo of God's voice. The right was but the record of God's will. A personal and living Being, a faithful and present Friend, was the power which made conscience, the right, duty, all that they were to those Christian heroes. So it will always be with men in whom religion assumes the solidity of a principle. Only as God energizes it, can religion take on a form so grand and so abiding.

4. The religion of principle is *the only type of religious character which commands the confidence of the world.* Who would have predicted that three

young men, but a little above the age and rank of boys, waifs from a foreign land and a subject people, exposed at any moment to the penalty of death, should win over to a new and despised religion the respect of the haughtiest monarch of the East? Yet this was the fruit of their daring defiance of his commands. His outraged pride was awed by their fidelity to a principle. "Blessed be the God of Shadrach, Meshach, and Abednego! There is no God that can deliver after this sort. His servants have yielded their bodies, that they might not worship any god but their own God." Such is the outburst of astonished conviction from the awe-struck king.

Always and everywhere men fall back and give place to those who practise a religion which costs them something. Other sorts of religion there are which serve their turn in idle hours and times of ease. There is a religion of form, whose pageantries please the eye, and which does well enough for a religion of state on festive days. There is a religion of taste, in which music and architecture, and the poetry of a painted window, may charm the fancy of culture and refinement, when no great stress of real life is upon them. There is a religion of feeling, which may uplift great assemblies on great occasions, and bear them on waves of religiosity which to certain temperaments may seem for the time to mount up to the gates of heaven.

These reflections and refractions of religion in times of prosperity, when no emergency tries the souls of men, may do very well for their religious entertainment, and the quieting of religious fears. But when the tug of real life comes, when temptation, bereavement, disappointment, disease, death, bring men's religion to the proof, these religious fictions vanish in thin air. No religious plaything answers the purpose then. Men feel then the need of something real, something solid, something profound, something godlike.

Similar is the power of a religion of principle, when viewed as a spectacle by reverent observers. Nothing else rouses the enthusiasm of lookers-on, and brings out their huzzas to the echo, like a grand spectacle of self-sacrifice to a religious principle on a grand scale.

In 1843 the Free Church of Scotland left the shelter of the State Establishment. Four hundred and seventy-five clergymen gave up their stipends, the principal of which amounted to two millions of pounds sterling. They abandoned the dignity of association with a great empire. They left behind them the parishes in which they and their fathers had labored, the churches in which they were baptized, the Lord's table at which they had ministered, the manses where their children had been born and in which they had hoped to die. From almost all that was dear to them on earth, they went out, and cast themselves on their fidelity to each other and the promises of God. Some of them had to worship on the sea-beach at low tide, because the noble landlords would not sell or lease a foot of land for a dissenting chapel. All this for *one* principle of religious faith, which in conscience they could not surrender, and would not dishonor.

Among their ablest opponents was the Hon. Judge Jeffrey, an ornament to the judiciary of Scotland, and one of the shining lights of her literature. He had spoken against them, argued against them, written against them, ridiculed their scruples to the last, and had predicted, that, to a man, they would yield if the trial came. The trial did come, and they did not yield. The ejected pastors quietly laid their protest before Lord Bute, who was present in the General Assembly as the representative of the Crown; then turned, and in solemn silence left the reverend judicature in which some of them had sat as leaders for many years, but whose dignities they were to enjoy no more.

As they filed out of the house, and marched down the High Street of Edinburgh, with the venerable Chalmers — the foremost man of all Scotland — at their head, Judge Jeffrey was told by a friend, who came rushing in to inform him. "They are out! They are out!" — "Who are out?" — "The evangelicals. There they go down High Street. Don't you hear the cheers of the crowd?" The august judge sprang to his feet, and, swinging his hat in the air with a huzza as hearty as the loudest, he cried out, "Three cheers for old Scotland! Nowhere out of Scotland could so grand a thing have happened!"

Yes, indeed, my lord, everywhere sacrifice to a religion of principle is a grand thing. Everywhere, in Scotland or out, it can be done, and nowhere without commanding the ovations of lookers-on, friend or foe. Something in the human hearts of us all exults in it. Tears of joy come in the telling of it. Men not capable of it themselves approve it, trust it, revere it. It is the only thing in the shape of religion which they do trust under all conditions and at all times.

Is not this the type of religion which the world needs to witness, above all things else, to-day? Not only in great exigencies and in sympathizing crowds. No, not in these mainly. But in still, private life, and in the dull round of individual toil. We have religious enthusiasm in great assemblies, enough and to spare. We have great religious awakenings in abundance, in which the numbers of the church swell by myriads. We have great religious organizations, societies, institutions, in which we glory, and into whose treasuries the wealth of nations flows. Our religion, in these developments of its social and literary and missionary power, thrives, never more than in these times of ours.

But there is a calm and even flow of religious

principle in the individual, which underlies all these, and which vitalizes them all. That is the thing which needs re-enforcement and revival. Does not the world's conversion drag for the want of this? Does not the faith of the world in the reality of our religion falter for the want of it? Men look to see religion in the life. They look to see Christian merchants carrying their faith to their counting-rooms; Christian lawyers, theirs before juries; Christian mechanics, theirs to their workshops; Christian fathers and mothers, theirs to their homes, under the honest eyes of children, and the silent criticism of servants. They are looking to see Christian leaders of society applying their religion to the settlement of questions of social caste, and the choice of the churches in which they shall worship; to see Christian ministers carrying theirs into private life in the selection of places of professional labor, in the subordination of salaries to usefulness, of dignities to souls, of literary tastes to missionary toils, of diplomacy to godly sincerity.

Trades, professions, households, social usages, the uses of property, the limits of its increase, amusements, schools, travels, — the world is waiting to see all these Christianized when in Christian hands, — Christianized in the sense of being made Christ*like* in the principles which govern them. It is looking on to see if ours is a religion *which costs us any thing*. Do we really feel the sacrifice of any one thing for Christ? Does our life unmistakably and inevitably remind men of Christ's life? Does it probably remind *him* of it? Does he see in it of the travail of his soul that which satisfies him?

This is the style of questioning by which the world is silently putting our religion to the test. One revival of a religion of such *costly* principle, pervading individual life, would be worth a thousand revivals of religious emotion and prayer and song, in packed assemblies, if they stop there.

Yet how easy it is to talk in this strain! Let us who talk it, live it! One of the early Presbyterian ministers of Virginia once said, at the close of one of his most pungent sermons of reproof, "O my soul, hear thou this word! for I must preach to the *one* who needs it most."

THE MAN IN THE LIONS' DEN.

Then said Daniel unto the king, O king, live forever. My God hath sent his angel, and hath shut the lions' mouths, that they have not hurt me: forasmuch as before him innocency was found in me; and also before thee, O king, have I done no hurt. Then was the king exceeding glad for him, and commanded that they should take Daniel up out of the den. So Daniel was taken up out of the den; and no manner of hurt was found upon him, because he believed in his God. — DAN. vi. 21-23.

DO not some of us remember the rude woodcut of "Daniel among the Lions," which seemed such a marvel of art to us in our childhood? We marvelled at the courage of the man of God in putting his arm calmly around the neck of the lion in the foreground. Would he do it if he stood in front, where we did, and saw the grim look of the beast face to face? We doubted. That one in the rear, — surely he was creeping up like a cat from behind, all ready to spring upon his victim. Such is the struggle of faith with sight. Angels are nowhere in the comparison with lions.

More than a lifetime of a generation has passed with some of us since our faith and our fancy first wrestled over the story; yet is it not to-day as fresh as ever? Let us see how it reads to our maturer wisdom.

1. The story illustrates the fact *that God often seems to crown the machinations of the wicked against the good with success.* Daniel was the victim of a conspiracy. His very virtues were the spring of the trap laid to catch him in an act of treason. His enemies knew their man. They knew that he would be true to his religion, come life, come death. The plot was adroit. It was executed to the letter. To all appearance it was successful. When that stone closed over the mouth of that den, his enemies had good reason to exult in the assurance that they had seen the last of him. They slept that night with grim pleasure in their dreams, at the thought that beasts were crunching his bones.

Such is sometimes God's way of procedure. He gives wicked men full swing. He does not interfere early in the beginnings of wrong. Not till the plot has ripened, the victim been insnared, the den opened, and the stone rolled over his head, does the angel of rescue step in. Many times over has this been the story of persecution. The blackest feature in the history of persecutors is their fiendish joy at the suffering of other men; and the darkest mystery in God's dealing with them is that the malign pleasure which they show does not provoke God to destroy them.

Claverhouse, the persecutor of the Covenanters,

used to witness, smiling, the agony of his victims in torture by the thumbscrew and the "boots." The "Blood Council," in the Netherlands, used to celebrate their wholesale executions by midnight carousals. One of the persecuting kings of England used to order decapitations to be executed before the windows, in sight of his guests at the dinner-table. He sought to give a relish to the royal dessert by the thud of the executioner's axe. He drank to the health of the victim who begged for one hour's reprieve. So secure, so free from trepidation, so oblivious of an avenging God, have wicked men often felt, at the height of their success, in doing the work of devils.

Time was when the torturing and burning of live men was a branch of ordinary and respectable business. Men chose it as a trade, and got their living out of it. The items of the process used to be entered in a ledger, like a grocer's bill. Mr. Motley, the historian, quotes the following from the old account-book of a Spanish executioner, the original of which he found in the Spanish archives: —

To Jacques Barra, Dr.

For torturing twice John de Lannoy	10 sous.
For executing said Lannoy by fire	60 sous.
For throwing his remains into the river	8 sous.

With such diabolical coolness do satanic men execute their will upon the friends of God. And God lets them do it. Oh, poor John de Lannoy!

Was there no being in the universe to whom thine agony in the fire was worth more than *fifty-seven cents?* and thy pains on the rack, once and again, more than *nine cents and a half?*

2. The story of the man in the den illustrates, also, *the insidiousness of sin in drawing men into extremes of guilt which they never planned for.* Darius was personally no enemy to Daniel. The prophet was his favorite minister, rather. The king was overreached as well as the victim. The conspiracy was so laid as to compel him, from motives of state policy, to execute the vindictive law against the first statesman of the realm. He passed a sleepless night, as many another overreached sinner has done, in unavailing repentance.

Most truthful is the whole scene to the facts of real life. Sin creates sin. Beginning in vanity, it ends in remorse. A little rivulet swells to an Amazon. A man can never do one wrong thing, and with dignity stop there. Factitious laws of honor, claims of usage, bonds of habit, hedge him around, press him down, and crowd him on to deeper crime. Duellists have shed blood murderously before God and their own consciences, who still seemed to themselves to be unwilling murderers. The most stupendous guilt man ever incurred has come upon him under stress of a tyranny of circumstance which he himself invited.

Such was the sin of Pontius Pilate. Well has an old English poet represented him as sunk beneath the waves, with nothing visible but his hands, and these washing themselves eternally, in vain attempt to cleanse his soul, and exclaiming, lifting up his head, —

> "I Pilate am: the falsest judge, alas!
> And most unjust, that by unrighteous
> And wicked doom, to Jews despiteous,
> Delivered up the Lord of life, to die!"

Such is the trap of doom into which sin allures its victims. Probably the lost sinner never yet lived who planned the end of his career at its beginning. " Is thy servant a dog, that he should do this thing?" Yet he did the thing. Yes, he was a dog. Penitentiaries are filled with men who seem to themselves to have drifted there on the resistless tide of little sins swollen into great sins. Murderers have swung on scaffolds, who said they were victims rather than criminals. Hell is populous with such victims. Said Alexander Hamilton, when dying on the duelling-ground by the shot of Aaron Burr, "I die like a fool." So he did. It is the way of sin to make men fools. The greater the man, the greater the fool.

3. This story of the man and the lions illustrates, further, *the supremacy of duty over intrigue in the defence of the right*. The great statesman of Babylon fell before duplicity and stratagem. Yet the work of his defence was not of that sort. He did not try to outwit intrigue by intrigue.

His was a much more simple and safe procedure. He had simply to do right. He said his prayers "as he did aforetime." He prayed kneeling, as he had always done. He prayed aloud, as had been his wont. Three times a day, and with windows open, he called on the God of his fathers, as his mother had taught him in his boyhood.

A more adroit man would have practised casuistry upon himself. A diplomatic saint would have shut his window, drawn a curtain, prayed in a whisper, lessened the number of his devotions, had some other engagement, if haply he might thus have saved his quivering limbs from the lions' teeth. Not so this simple child of God. He was no Jesuit. He would not save life or limb by any Machiavellian policy. Not so much as by the lowering of his voice or the closing of a shutter would he seem to fear man more than God.

Such is the grandeur of duty. A simple thing. A child can understand it: a dying man can do it. Yet the diplomacy of courts and cabinets, backed by the standing armies of the world, is no match for it. Lay it down as a first principle of truth, *that, if a man will take care of the right, God will take care of him.* In the long-run, and as a general rule, there is no such thing as a good man's failure. He may suffer: the right deserves that sacrifice. He may die: the right is worthy of that cost. But he cannot fail. God will look out for that. As a general rule, the drift of things, even in this world, is such that good men succeed by simply doing right. The weakest thing in this world is a stratagem when offset by a straightforward act of duty by a live man. On the contrary, it will commonly be found that in the exceptional case in which a good man does fail, his failure is nearly in proportion to the extent to which intrigue has entered into his plans of procedure. Men of stratagem in God's service are not, as a rule, successful men. Men of wily conscience are not the men of heaviest weight. They are not the men who turn the scales of things in crises. They are never safe leaders, nor the best men.

4. I am indebted to one of the most suggestive of recent commentators on the text, for the striking hint that the story of Daniel illustrates *the need which human governments often experience, of something like an atonement for the violation of law.* This Eastern despot acted under stress of what he deemed the dignity of law. Chaldæan jurisprudence provided no way for what we should call the *constitutional* pardon of a transgressor. Once proved guilty, he must suffer, no matter what his rank or the palliations of his crime. It was a clear case of conflict between mercy and legal justice.

Other human governments experience the same conflict. The great anomaly of human administration of law is the power of pardon. Law, as such, knows nothing of it. Be the pressure on the side of mercy ever so great, Law says, "Pardon! What is that?" In modern governments, we jump the difficulty by lodging the power of pardon somewhere, ignoring law. Yet never is that power exercised without loss to the prestige of authority. Murderers take courage in crime for every murderer who escapes the scaffold.

Well-known cases have occurred in which the benevolent impulses of an entire people were all one way, and the necessities of law were all the other way; and benevolence was impotent, and law triumphant.

Such was the conflict between justice and mercy, when Major André, the British spy, was condemned to death by the American court-martial. Probably Washington never set his hand to a document which cost him a more severe struggle than that caused by the death-warrant of André. But the safety of our young Republic would not permit the deed of mercy. Its very life hung in a trembling scale. Twenty Arnolds might have been the fruit of pardoning one André. Therefore said the commander-in-chief, "He is a spy. By the laws in war, his life is forfeit. He must die." And die he did.

In all such instances, human governments betray their need of something equivalent to an *atonement!* something to do for human law what the atonement of Christ does for the laws of God in the pardon of the guilty. In that still moment in which men hold their breath, in waiting to hear the death-sentence from the judge, he bows his head, and weeps for some other way of vindicating the eternal sacredness of law than by the doom of the now trembling offender. Is there no other sacrifice, in earth or heaven, which will take its place? What else was the meaning of the tears and the faltering voice with which Chief-Justice Shaw of Massachusetts pronounced sentence of death upon his friend Professor Webster?

The argument, therefore, from real life, is to this point: Why should not the same necessity be felt under the government of God? Why should we believe that the mind of the universe could bear without moral anarchy the shock of the wholesale pardon of sin, when the mind of man cannot bear the shock which law suffers in the pardon of one poor, tempted brother-man? Why should we not believe that infinite justice feels the need of some device for the protection of its sacredness, when a world of criminals goes free? And why should we not believe, on the authority of God's word, that infinite wisdom has found it in the device of an atonement by the sinless yet dying Son of God?

5. The story of the man in the den suggests yet further, that *God's deliverance of the good is often by methods in which the marvellous borders upon the*

miraculous. The closing of the lion's mouth for the safety of the prophet was a miracle. What, then, can we learn from this feature of the story? Not that we are to look for miraculous interventions in our behalf. Not that we are to expect angels to come to our rescue from wild beasts and wilder men. The principle which governs God's interference with the natural and probable course of things is this, — that he will do for us what he sees, in his infinite insight and foresight, to be best, all *things* considered, and for all *persons* concerned; and that in doing this he often achieves results which are as distinctly suggestive of his agency as miracles are. In such deliverances, devout minds will see God as clearly as if he spoke audibly from the heavens, or as if one heard the wings of angels rustling in the air.

The story of the lions in the den recalls incidents very like it in the experience of African travellers. Mungo Park once found himself confronted by a raging lion, against which he had no other available weapon than the look of his *eye.* Yet the beast which had, a moment before, come bounding and roaring towards him, stopped suddenly, looked abashed upon the ground, and then turned and slunk away.

Another traveller in African wilds was once actually seized by a hungry lion, thrown to the ground, and had begun to feel the mysterious anæsthesia which the magnetism of wild beasts is said to produce in their victims, when suddenly opening his eyes, and fixing them steadily on the eye of the beast, he saw that its bloodshot look wavered. The soul of the beast recognized the soul of its natural lord. He let go his hold on the prostrate man, turned with tail between his legs, and fled.

In these cases there was no miracle. But were those saved victims idiots in kneeling there on the desert, and offering up thanks to an unseen power? Marvel or miracle, it matters little what we call it, the agency of God in such events is beyond question. Whether he works by a miraculous *suspension* of the laws of nature, or by a marvellous *use* of those laws, what matters that? Sufficient is it that he makes himself known to us as a very present help in our emergency.

With such tokens of God's presence, does not every human life abound? I know a man who believes that he was once wakened by a supernatural influence from slumber, at the critical moment, in time to save his child from his burning dwelling. One moment more, and it would have been too late. Another believes that by an unaccountable impression upon his mind he was turned back from a journey to his home, to save his family from nocturnal burglars. Another was so beset by providential hinderances as to prevent his embarking on board a ship which was never heard of after leaving port. President Lincoln believed that he was forewarned of some great catastrophe a night or two before his death. The last day of his life he spent under the shadow of eternity. Who of us does not know of such events, which, if they were woven into a romance, the world would pronounce unnatural, if not absurd? Yet who of us can help believing? Yes, in every human life, truth *is* stranger than fiction.

6. The story of Daniel illustrates, finally, the fact that *the rescue of the good often involves the destruction of the wicked, by a very subtle law which may be called the law of retributive re-action.* The enemies of the prophet-statesman fell when he was restored. The scales were held by an even and steady hand. When one went up, the other went down. Though the revulsion came about by the caprice of a despot, yet God *used* that caprice as the motor to the execution of a profound law which often appears in his administration of the world. Providential retribution, upon ungodly nations, occurs largely in the way of re-action from the oppression of the good by the violence and the machinations of the wicked. The destinies of the good and the bad are so bound up together, that the salvation of the one is often by necessary sequence the doom of the other. A late writer has said that the most *characteristic* thing which this world has to show to other worlds is a scaffold on the morning of an execution. What for, but for the stress which the

security of the innocent lays upon law to afflict the guilty?

Do we not remember how our childish sense of retributive justice responded approvingly to the story as it ran: that "the lions had the mastery" of those bad men, and "brake all their bones in pieces or ever they came to the bottom of the den"? We did not know our feeling by any high-sounding philosophic title. "Retributive justice" we knew nothing about; but did we not put the case to the same purpose in our childish way, saying, "It served them right"? Were we not sensible of a mysterious satisfaction, down deep within us, which our unsophisticated conscience did not call cruelty? Children are not by nature believers in the doctrine of universal salvation.

Turn, then, the argument to the mystery of an eternal hell. How do we know that the safety of the good in eternity, and throughout the universe of peopled space, does not involve, by this law of retributive re-action, the punishment of the wicked? How do we know that heaven and hell are not so bound together in the meshes of moral government over free beings, that the one cannot exist without the other?

Sin matured, be it remembered, is no longer the silken and polite depravity which for the most part it assumes to be in this world. It takes on the form of demoniacal hostility to God and to all holy beings. Consolidated in that mould of malign character, it voluntarily *chooses* to remain forever. It is energized by spiritual powers of which we in the body have no conception. We do not know what resources of temptation, of guile, of direct assault and resistless conquest, may be inherent in the very nature of a lost soul, set free from the limitations of a sensuous body. Whatever the soul might have been as an heir of heaven, so great it must be, perhaps, as an heir of hell. The possibilities of spiritual being are the same, measured either way. Whatever its resources are, the lost soul holds them at the service of eternal sin. Heaven has once been thrown into consternation by them. Angels kept not their first estate. There was war in heaven. Have you ever realized in your imagination the possibilities of satanic revolution through the universe, involved in that one fact of an angelic fall?

The practical question, therefore, as it must present itself to the diplomacy of infinite wisdom in adjusting the government of the universe, is this: Shall devils and devilish men be let loose to prey upon the objects of their hate forever? Shall heaven itself become hell? Is there not in all our hearts an instinct of upspringing and iron-hearted justice which, if the security of the good requires, by the law of retributive re-action, the eternal confinement of the incorrigibly wicked, says in mournful and tender, yet firm and satisfied rejoinder, "Amen and amen"? Did not St. John hear something like this, when he saw "the smoke of torment ascending forever"? "I heard a great voice of much people in heaven saying, Alleluia! For true and righteous are thy judgments. And again they said, Alleluia! And the smoke of her torment rose up for ever and ever."

We are often asked, "How can you *bear* to believe in an eternal hell? Why does it not craze you? How can you call such a God as can create a hell, benevolent? To us he seems satanic in his nature. Yes, your God is my Devil."

Whenever I go from my home to the city of Boston, I pass by a building which reminds me of the castle of Giant Despair. It is constructed of heavy granite blocks to the very roof. It is surrounded with lofty granite walls, and these are surmounted with iron spikes. I see doors of massive iron riveted with iron bolts. I see windows barred with iron. Behind those iron bars, I have seen pale, despairing human faces, — faces which have re-appeared to me in my dreams. I know that underneath those walls, in a dungeon cell, there lives a man, manacled hand and foot, who has clanked his chains there for seventeen years. Sometimes more than five hundred of my human brothers are locked within those walls of living death.

I have been told that over against a certain window there, on the opposite side of the street, there lives a pale-faced woman who never smiles. Every morning she places on her window-sill a blooming flower, where a certain man behind those bars can see it, and can know that a loving woman is thinking of him. Yet I see, in a turret on those walls, a man in uniform, with a rifle at his shoulder, who, if he sees that brother man trying to clamber over the walls, and touch the hand of that loving woman, is instructed to shoot him down like a dog.

Why do I not cry out against the malign power which keeps asunder that suffering wife and husband? Why do I not tramp the streets of Boston, pleading with the crowds to go with me, and level that Bastille to the ground? Why do I not move heaven and earth against the infernal tyranny which has devised, and the cold-hearted cruelty which tolerates, that granite hell? What is it that sustains my humane sensibilities and yours at the sight of such an anomaly of despair, in a world where robins are singing in the spring-time, and violets are blooming on the hillsides, and little children are laughing in their glee?

Answer me this, and I will tell you what it is that sustains a benevolent universe in beholding, and a benignant God in devising, an *eternal* hell for the confinement of *eternal* guilt. And you must prove to me that it is *not* so, before you can charge God with satanic wrong in tolerating such a place as hell within the bounds of his dominions.

The question which all such suspicions of God's

rectitude bring back like a boomerang upon the inquirer is, What *else* shall God do with eternal guilt? Shall he forgive it? Shall he, by one grand act of amnesty, proclaim liberty to the damned, to the Devil, to his angels, and to men like them? But how would that help the matter, sin remaining unrepented of and unforsaken? Free grace proclaimed in hell forever would not quench for one moment its lurid fires, if sin were still regnant there. Sin is hell. "Myself am hell," says Milton's Satan. Guilt is itself damnation. Again the question returns therefore: "What else shall God do with it?"

Shall he give repentance, and then forgive? But that is the very thing he has been offering from the first. Never will man or devil see the moment when he cannot repent if he would. But that is the very thing from which the incorrigible sinner recoils. He will have none of that. Repentance means submission. Better hell than that. Such is the relentless *choice* of the doomed one. Doomed because self-doomed. Doomed by the fearful omnipotence of his own free-will. Nothing else which it is in God's power to offer does he spurn from him with such concentration of obdurate and vindictive resolve. His whole being revolts from it with the intensity, at last, of ages of accumulated and malign passion.

Such is SIN: once chosen and implanted and indurated in the very nature of man, by a life of abused probation, in which the grace of God has been scorned, and the blood of Christ outraged. Once more, then, the question comes back unanswered: "What else shall God do with it?" Through all eternity, that is the question which infinite benevolence will ask of an awe-struck yet satisfied and adoring universe: "*What else shall God do with it?*"

THE FULFILMENT OF PROPHECY IN THE CAREER OF CYRUS.

> Now in the first year of Cyrus, king of Persia, that the word of the Lord spoken by the mouth of Jeremiah might be accomplished, the Lord stirred up the spirit of Cyrus, king of Persia, that he made a proclamation throughout all his kingdom, and put it also in writing. . . . Thus saith Cyrus, king of Persia, All the kingdoms of the earth hath the Lord God of heaven given me; and he hath charged me to build him a house in Jerusalem, which is in Judah. Who is there among you of all his people? The Lord his God be with him, and let him go up. — 2 CHRON. xxxvi. 22, 23.

AN eminent Jewish scholar once read for his entertainment the Gospel of Matthew. As he read, his curiosity deepened into a more solemn interest. A second time he read it, and his face grew pale. The closing scenes in the life of our Lord enchained his attention as never before. When he read for the third time of the death and burial of Christ, he dashed the book across the room, exclaiming with an oath, "Yes, the story is true! The cursed Nazarene was the Messiah of the prophets." The evidence which had convinced him against his will was the exactness with which the biography of Jesus tallied with the prophecy of Isaiah, written seven hundred years before.

The fulfilment of prophecy is one of the two supernatural arguments for the truth of the Scriptures. I can think of no more valuable use which I can make of this portion of Holy Scripture than to present in some detail the fulfilment of prophecy in the career and conquests of Cyrus. If my young readers will have patience to follow me into some of the minute declarations of Isaiah, I think they will be rewarded by information which may be of lifelong value to them.

In order to appreciate the comparison of the prophecy with the history, it is necessary to observe, as a preliminary, that Isaiah wrote not less than a hundred and thirty years before Cyrus was born, and not less than a hundred and fifty years before his conquest of Babylon. It was long before the Median kingdom existed. The captivity of Judah had not begun. Three or four generations lived and died between the prophet and the Persian prince. The prophet could not possibly have other means of knowing who Cyrus was to be, or what he was to do in the world, than the simple revelation of the facts by the Spirit of God. Yet that he foretold the conqueror's career, down to minutest details, is established by precisely the same kind and amount of evidence which proves that either Cyrus or Isaiah existed at all. Bear this in mind as we go on with the story.

What, then, does the prophet tell us of the Persian hero, which history confirms? The following are the most singular coincidences between the two: —

1. The *name* of Cyrus, the point of the compass indicative of his *birthplace*, and the *direction of his march upon Babylon*, are distinctly foretold. "Thus saith the Lord to *Cyrus*. I have raised up one from the *north*. From the rising of the sun — that is, from the *east* — shall he call upon my name." The two points of the compass named in this language of Isaiah are singularly true. Cyrus was born in Persia, which was east of Babylon. It was commonly called "the East." One historian speaks of it as the "land of the sun-rising." But at a very early age Cyrus was removed to Media, lying on the north of Babylon; and it was from Media that he came down at the head of victorious hosts upon the doomed capital. The prophet thus sees in a vision a prince of *eastern* birth, marching upon the city from the *north*, and that his name is *Cyrus*.

Small matters these, but all the more significant for that. The question is, Who told Isaiah such minute details about a man he never saw or heard of; coming from a kingdom which at that time had no existence; achieving a conquest which then had not been dreamed of? How did he know what name the future conqueror would bear, a hundred and thirty years before he had a name?

Did anybody ever predict Bonaparte's conquest of Italy a century before his birth? Did ever statesman or magician, as far back as A. D. 1650, declare, that, a century and a half later, a conqueror born in the west of Italy would come down from the north, and take possession of Rome, and that his name would be Napoleon? Yet this is in kind what the Hebrew prophet did. The question is, who told him all that? How did he alone, of all the inhabitants of the world, find out the facts so exactly and so minutely?

2. Isaiah furthermore describes with remarkable accuracy *the personal character of Cyrus*. His warlike spirit, his towering ambition, the rapidity of his conquests, the equity of his administration, and his heathen religion, are all declared, after the manner of prophecy. "Calling a *ravenous bird* from the East," is the prophet's language. Prophetic vision deals largely in symbols. The eagle is its favorite symbol of an aspiring, warlike, swift conqueror. "Who raised up the *righteous man* from the East," is the prophetic description of Cyrus. It is almost the exact language in which historians describe the government of the Persian king. "The just one," he is often called. "Take example from the Persian," the tutors of Oriental princes used to say to their royal pupils. "I have girded thee, though thou hast not known me," are the words which prophecy puts into the mouth of God concerning him.

This is a distinct prediction of his ignorance of the true God.

These are but a few specimens of the prophetic touches of which there are many more, portraying with an artist's skill the character of this monarch. Imagine now, that, in addition to announcing the name and the birthplace of Napoleon a hundred and thirty years before he was born, the magician had described him as an eagle in his conquests; had said that he would originate a superior code of jurisprudence, — the "Code Napoleon;" and that in his religion he would be a Romanist. Would not such hints, *added* to the items before named, redouble the surprise at the magician's power? Would not men ask with astonishment who he was, where he came from, by whose authority he spoke, and where he got his information? Yet this is just what Isaiah declares of the great conqueror of the East.

3. The significance of the prophecy deepens, when it comes to describe *the conquests achieved by Cyrus*. Passages abound of which these are specimens: "He gave the nations before him. He made him ruler over kings. He made them as dust to his sword, and as driven stubble to his bow. The isles saw it, and feared: they helped every one his neighbor. Every one said to his neighbor, Be of good courage. I will subdue nations under him. I will loose the loins of kings."

By such rapid glances, the half of which I do not quote, the prophet foretells the victories of Cyrus over the great nations of the East; the consternation of their kings; their alliances for mutual defence; and the velocity with which the Persian legions marched from victory to victory.

Turn we now to history: what has that to say? It does but repeat the prophecy in describing the facts as they occurred. Says one, "He had scarcely gained one victory, before his tumultuous forces poured down on other battle-grounds. Scarcely had one city fallen, before he stood thundering at the gates of another. Empires were like dust before him, and cities like chaff." That prophecy, "*I* will loose the loins of kings," had its exact fulfilment in the consternation of Belshazzar at the handwriting on the wall, when the Persian armies were on the march, and within twenty-four hours would be heard tramping the streets of the doomed capital.

4. The prophecy of *the downfall of Babylon deserves distinct review*. The prophetic story runs in this style: "Evil shall come upon thee. Thou shalt not know from whence it riseth. Thou shalt not be able to put it off. Desolation shall come suddenly, which thou shalt not know." Thus is expressed the sudden, the unexpected, the irresistible, and the *improbable* calamity, which was coming upon that haughty city.

Just such, in fact, was its conquest by Cyrus.

That event, to begin with, was in itself, and in any form, improbable. The military science of the age pronounced Babylon impregnable by any methods of assault or siege then known. So secure did king and people feel that it could not be taken by human force or strategy, that, on the very night of its capture by Cyrus, they were given up to feasting and carousal behind their insurmountable walls. The king would not believe the rumor of the enemy's entrance, even when the blood of his people was flowing in the streets.

Here, again, little incidents are detailed, which no soothsayer would have thought of, or would have dared to predict if he had thought of them. "I will say to the deep, Be dry; I will dry up thy rivers. I will open before him the two-leaved gates. The gates shall not be shut." The significance of this language will appear from arraying it side by side with the historic facts. Babylon was a city fifteen miles square. It was intersected by the river Euphrates, as London is by the Thames, and Paris by the Seine, and Philadelphia by the Schuylkill. Solid walls surrounded it, three hundred and fifty feet high, and broad enough on the top for four chariots to be driven abreast. The two sections again were separated by walls running along both banks of the river. Fronting the streets on either side were folding gates for convenience of access to the stream by day, which the police were instructed to close at the setting of the sun.

Cyrus took the city by a remarkable stratagem. In military invention he was a genius. He strikingly resembled our own Gen. Sherman. In our late civil war Gen. Sherman once despatched a force to cross a certain river at a given point. His subordinates soon came back, saying that there was no bridge there, and that the river was not fordable for twenty miles. Said the general, with flashing eye, "Isn't there a village within five miles of there? " Yes, sir." — " Well, go back, and level every house in that village to the ground, and with the timbers *build* a bridge across the river." And they did it.

Cyrus was the Sherman of ancient warfare. His genius invented a novel way of marching his army into impregnable Babylon. If he could not march *over* the walls, he would contrive to march *under*. He did it by a very simple expedient, when once thought of, but only he had the genius to think of it. He dug an immense canal *around* the walls, and turned the river Euphrates into it. Then he marched his army at dead of night, and in dead silence, *under* the walls, in the vacant bed of the river. But this brought him only between the two other immense river-walls inside. How to surmount these was the question. The indomitable general had provided scaling-ladders for the purpose. But the God of Isaiah had done better

THE FULFILMENT OF PROPHECY. 303

for him than that. Sure enough, he found those gates which let the citizens down to the river in the day-time — "two-leaved," that is, folding gates — wide open. Like other drunken policemen, the custodians of Babylon had neglected to close those gates.

If my young readers have ever seen the gates which are used in the locks of a canal, like those of the Erie Canal at Little Falls, they will have some idea of the structure of the "two-leaved gates" of Babylon, and of the importance to an invading army, penned up in the channel of the Euphrates, of finding those gates open. Thus Cyrus found them. Even the palace-gates were not closed. The invader got near enough to hear the drunken carousals of the king and his courtiers inside, before they were convinced of his approach. Do you not now see a new meaning in the words? "I will dry up thy rivers; I will open the two-leaved gates; the gates shall not be shut; I will loose the loins of kings."

Herodotus, the ancient historian of the event, writing seventy years afterwards, comments upon it in this manner: "If the besieged had been aware of the designs of Cyrus, they might have destroyed his troops. They had only to secure the *folding gates* leading to the river, and to have manned the embankments on either side, and they would have enclosed the Persians in a trap from which they could never have escaped. *As it happened,* they were taken by surprise; and such is the extent of the city, that they who lived in the extremities were made prisoners before the alarm reached the palace." "As it happened." Yes, it happened; but, a hundred and more years before, God had said by his prophet *how* it should happen. He had said, "*I* will open the two-leaved gates." So Cyrus found them wide open, and the way clear to the very banquet-hall of the palace, just as Isaiah had said, before Cyrus was born, that they should be.

Now, suppose that about the time of the American Revolution, the Rev. Dr. Witherspoon, one of the signers of the Declaration of Independence from New Jersey, had fallen into a trance. Suppose that in that trance he had foreseen and declared that one *Sherman* would arise in distant times, who should go down from the *north*, and march from the *west* to the seaboard with a conquering army, scattering devastation on his way; that his march would be like the flight of an eagle; that city after city should fall before him; that consternation should fill the hearts of the people, and of the governors of States; and that by that march from victory to victory he should aid in putting an end to a civil war which threatened the existence of the nation, — suppose that in describing Sherman's march from Atlanta to Savannah, that incident of his building a bridge and crossing a river with the timbers of demolished houses were named in language which could mean nothing else, — would not the men of our time have reason to think Dr. Witherspoon, in his trance, had something more than guesswork in his prevision of the future?

Yet all this would not have been more singular, more improbable, more impossible to human view, than these predictions of Isaiah respecting the march of the Persian monarch to the conquest of Babylon. The question therefore returns, laden with redoubled significance, Where did Isaiah get his information? Who told him that Babylon, a hundred and fifty years afterwards, would be shut off from the Euphrates by gates? Who told him that they would be folding gates? How did he know that a man named Cyrus would enter the capital in the bed of the river, and on that particular night, contrary to usage and to law, would find that the police had left those gates open, as if on purpose to let the invader in? In short, how came he to write *history* a hundred and fifty years beforehand? Did any other historian ever write his history a century and a half before it happened, instead of a century and a half later, and be lucky enough to have it all happen to be true, even down to the structure and the opening of a gate?

5. One other feature of the prophecy and the history in parallels remains to be noticed. Isaiah explicitly foretells *the restoration of Judah from*

captivity, and the rebuilding of the temple at Jerusalem, through the agency of Cyrus. God declares by the mouth of the prophet: " I will direct all his ways; . . . he shall let go my captives." " Even saying to Jerusalem, Be built; and to the temple, Thy foundations shall be laid." . . . " He shall let go my captives, not for price nor reward." " Ye shall be redeemed without money." . . . " Ye shall not go out with haste, nor go by flight."

Here we find another group of details which no uninspired mind could have guessed at, and no soothsayer would have dared to predict. Every one of them was to the last degree improbable. No statesman of the age did conjecture them. In the prophet's time, there were no captives at all in Babylon from Judah. When they became captives, long after, it was improbable that they would be released in any way by an Oriental despot, flushed with victory. They were very valuable captives. They were of an intelligent race. Good servants, able-bodied men and women for household use, skilful artisans, honest laborers, were abundant among them. Men of learning and genius, like Daniel, some of whom were deservedly advanced to high places in the realm, were Hebrews.

Scarcely any other race has the world ever found so serviceable as that despised stock of Abraham. At the very time when the Spanish Inquisition was persecuting the Jewish people to the death, and but one country in Europe was a safe asylum for them, many of the most eminent scholars, scientists, professors, musicians, even statesmen at the head of empires, were Jews in secret, living under assumed Gentile names. And to this day they are a race everywhere spoken against, but everywhere *used*. Not a great war can be carried on in Europe without the permission of a Jew. Bismarck, Andrassy, Gortschakoff, all are compelled to ask leave of a Jew before they dare to plunge the governments they represent into the vast expenditures caused by a great war. Lord Beaconsfield of England is himself a Jew.

So in the Persian economy: never was a more valuable class of slaves of equal number held by the rights of war than those held under command of Cyrus from Judæa. It was the last thing to be expected from an Eastern despot, that he should let such a people go free; that he should charge no ransom for them; that they should not be compelled to take their freedom by force or stratagem; that their master himself should restore to them their plundered treasures, and direct the rebuilding of their desolated temple. Never was a prediction more improbable on the face of it.

Yet all these things happened just as Isaiah said they would. The truth of the history no infidel presumes to question, whatever he may think of the prophecy. Imagine now, that a hundred years ago there had been no Africans in the

American colonies of Great Britain. Yet imagine that Dr. Witherspoon in his trance had declared that the march of one Sherman, the man of eagle eye, from the Cumberland to the seacoast, should result in the liberation of millions of African slaves; that they should go free suddenly; that not a dollar would be paid for their ransom; that they would not force their liberty by insurrection, nor steal it by flight; that it would be given to them outright by the proclamation of the president; and that in the city of Washington a grand university would be erected for their training as free citizens of the republic.

The men of that age might well have laughed at ravings so improbable. But what would now be the verdict of the men of our age? Should we believe that the story was all guesswork? Should we not believe that supernatural prescience was in it? Yet just such in kind was the vision of Isaiah, — no less specific in detail, no less consistent in the continuity of the story, and no less true to fact. Not the half of the coincidences between the prophecy and the history are given here. The prophecy now *all* reads like history. The facts of the one tally exactly with the prescience of the other.

The question therefore returns again, — How did Isaiah get his knowledge of coming events? Who told him *facts* a hundred and more years before the wisest statesman of the age had once thought of them as *conjectures?* Did any other man, not inspired of God, ever coin history thus out of guesswork? Did ever romance fall true like this? Sir Walter Scott wrote historical romances. Has "Ivanhoe" or "Quentin Durward" ever come true? Toss up a font of alphabetic type at random in the air, and will they come down all set and ready for the press in the form of the "Arabian Nights"? Yet this is, in substance, what infidelity asks us to believe, when it denies the gift of divine inspiration to the Hebrew prophets.

Such, then, is the argument from fulfilled prophecy for the divine origin of the Scriptures. The career of Cyrus is but a single sample. Other cases of the same kind swell the proof to volumes. The present condition of Babylon; the destruction of Moab; the fall of Tyre; the conquest of Egypt; the doom of Damascus; the desolation of Idumæa; the sack of Jerusalem; the life, death, and burial of Christ, — are events which belong to the same class. They all abound with the same sort of coincidence between the prophecy and the history. The coincidence extends to minute details. It is sustained without a break through long-continued narrative, covering years — yes, centuries, — and involving the destiny of individuals with the fate of nations and of empires.

Such intricate and involved prevision no human mind could have painted without a break in the truthfulness of the story, unless inspired by an omniscient God. Any other solution of the mystery throws upon us a weight of credulity a hundred-fold greater than that of faith in the "Arabian Nights" as authentic history. For the most part infidelity feels this, and very shrewdly decides to let the fulfilled prophecies of the Bible alone. There is no other argument for the truth of the Christian Scriptures, which infidels so generally agree to *ignore* as this.

A single admonition is suggested by this rapid review. It is, that young minds should *guard with special care against the beginnings of distrust in the divine origin of the Bible.* Any young man can be an infidel if he wills to be one. The Rev. Dr. Emmons was once appealed to by a saucy disbeliever in immortality, who said, "Show us the *evidence* of this thing you call a soul: what does it look like?" He replied, turning on his heel, "No: I can't prove a soul to a man who hasn't any."

So we cannot prove the divinity of the Bible to one who has no *will* to see it. But in a Christian land no man can deny it with an unsullied conscience. The evidence is clear; it is direct; it is abundant. Juries send men to the scaffold on evidence not the half of it. No man can resist it without guilt. No mind can sink so low, without approaching near to that state of matured depravity in which it calls evil good, and good evil;

truth falsehood, and falsehood truth; in which it believes absurdities, and trusts in contradictions, just because it stubbornly *wills* to do so.

Not the least among the surprises of the day of judgment will be the *re-discovery of lost truth*, through the resurrection of rejected evidence. Proofs which once men saw as in sunlight, but closed their eyes upon, will be again written in flaming fire. Eternity will be ablaze with them. These ancient Hebrew seers will be there, to bear witness to the evidence they left on record of the inspiration of God's word. "Fool that I was," will then be the verdict of many a lost being, — "fool that I was, not to *believe* what I *knew* to be true!"

The near approach of death sometimes anticipates the surprises of that day. Ethan Allen of Vermont, of Revolutionary fame as the leader of the "Green Mountain Boys," was an infidel. His wife was a devoted Christian. When he was on his death-bed he was asked, "Whose faith do you wish your children to adopt, yours or their mother's?" — "Their mother's," was the prompt reply.

A similar incident occurred in the last hours of the celebrated Dr. Paulus, professor of biblical literature at Heidelberg. He was substantially an atheist. He denied every thing supernatural, even to the denial of the immortality of the soul. When his fatal illness began, he declared that he was about to die, and that that would be the end of him. In this cheerless faith he calmly awaited the closing scene. When it came, he lay in a speechless coma for some hours. It was supposed that he would never speak again. But at last he suddenly opened his eyes, raised them to the ceiling, as if he saw something invisible to other than dying sight, and starting to raise himself in bed he exclaimed, "There *is* another life!" then fell back a corpse. What an appalling discovery to make at the last moment of an abused and lost probation! — that a man's lifelong faith, on which he has risked eternity, has been a lie, and that he has nothing now but the ruin of a soul to carry into another life. Let youthful readers take warning. Watch with prayer the first wavering beginning of distrust in the word of God.

It *is* the word of God. True or false, it is inspired by an omniscient mind. If false, it is a fraud so stupendous that mortal man could never have originated it. *The grandeur of the imposture would be as miraculous as its truth.* A living writer has declared that our Lord Jesus Christ was God, as he claimed to be, or he was the Devil. With unutterable reverence be the hypothesis tolerated for the moment. For it is between such extremes of best and worst that we have to choose in accepting or rejecting the religion of the Bible. There is no middle ground on which a reasonable man can stand, knowing nothing, believing nothing, caring nothing. This book is true, or it is a lie so stupendous that human thought never conceived it; and it comes to us sustained by evidences which to the common-sense of men must prove it to be the work of God. Which is the more probable? On which belief is it safer to risk eternity?

CHRIST THE CENTRE OF BIBLICAL THOUGHT.

I saw in the night visions, and, behold, one like the Son of man came with the clouds of heaven, and came to the Ancient of days, and they brought him near before him. And there was given him dominion, and glory, and a kingdom, that all people, nations, and languages, should serve him: his dominion is an everlasting dominion which shall not pass away, and his kingdom that which shall not be destroyed. — DAN. vii. 13, 14.

ONE of the first signs by which a traveller in Italy observes that he is approaching the capital of the kingdom, is that all the guide-boards bear its name. From whatever quarter of the compass he journeys, and by whatever highway, he sees at all corners the outstretched finger, and the words, "To Rome." The people have a proverb that "all roads lead to Rome."

Similar to this network of highways is the internal structure of the Bible. That, too, is covered over by lines of suggestion, which all point one way. They converge to one centre, and that centre is Christ. A sample of this is found in the text before us.

I. Let us first observe some of the details of

CHRIST THE CENTRE OF BIBLICAL THOUGHT. 315

biblical truth in which this centring of revelation in Christ is seen.

The first token of it which the reader of the Bible discovers is *the Old Testament doctrine of the Messiah*. From afar, back at the epoch of the fall, down to the last of the prophetic ages, we find the promise of the coming of a mysterious being, of miraculous birth and strange destiny. His life is to involve strange contradictions. He is to retrieve, in some mysterious way, the disaster of the fall. He is to engage in victorious conflict with the powers of darkness, and set men free from their dominion. Who he is, what he is, whence he is to come, what is to be his rank, what he is to do, how he is to live and how to die, are at first only hinted at. The seed of the woman shall bruise the head of the serpent. Then with increasing clearness comes the promise to Abraham. Then follow the types of the Mosaic ritual, pointing to a distant future, and hinting at an atoning tragedy. In the Psalms the great advent grows more resplendent: "Lo, I come: in the volume of the book it. is written of me." Finally the prophets pour forth a low and tender wail, as if chanting a funeral dirge over the despised and rejected One, the Man of sorrows; him whose visage was marred; in whom is no beauty; who should bear griefs not his own, and suffer stripes for others' healing. Then suddenly the scene changes, and the chorus swells and deepens into exulting and triumphal song of the Wonderful, the Counsellor, the Prince of peace, the mighty God, the everlasting Father. To a soul inquiring after God, the Old Testament seems to fill the air with these mysterious responses.

A German astronomer, not long ago, called my attention to the magnificent distances and the sublime evolutions of the heavenly bodies. Said he, "Up there in the December skies, I can see something that seems to me worthy of an almighty God. But when I come back from the stars to your Old-Testament story about fire coming down from the sky to burn up the fragments of a slaughtered lamb, it seems to me very petty in the contrast. I cannot help asking myself, 'What can the God of the sidereal universe have to do with that?'" True, it *is* very petty till we discover in the bleeding lamb, on the altars of Judæa, the symbol of the Lamb that was slain from the foundation of the world. It *is* beneath the notice of the God of the stars, until we discern in the blood of the sacrifice a type of the blood which was fore-ordained for the remission of sin before one star glistened in the diadem of night.

Take Christ out of the Old Testament, and the student of astronomy may well scorn and scout the whole story. Put back Christ into its pages, and they glow with a magnificence which the heaven of heavens cannot contain. Petty, is it?

CHRIST THE CENTRE OF BIBLICAL THOUGHT. 317

That very homeliness of its details is the measure of God's condescension. Thus he has come down to the slow and patient training of a rude people in a ruder age. Is the prattle of the nursery degrading to the young mother who fondly studies its meaning? What else marks the love of a mother like it? But for just such pettiness, what would the world have ever known of Homer and Plato? The Old Testament is simply the story of the moral nursery of the race. In this one fact lies the whole volume of reply to the carpings of infidelity.

The second feature of the Scriptures which exalts Christ as their central thought, is *the New-Testament doctrine of his sufferings and death.* Here, again, we find the same convergence of radii to a centre. Let a philosophical critic, unacquainted with Christian history, read the New Testament for the first time, and he cannot fail to see that the one central character of the whole is Christ. The central fact is the crucifixion. The locality of most intense significance is Calvary. The hero of the "Paradise Lost" is not so clearly defined as is the centring of the New-Testament thought in the person of Christ, and in his tragic death. As patriarch and prophets looked forward, so evangelists and apostles look backward, to this one mysterious person, and ponder the unfathomable significance of his dying words. Here is an event in the world's history, which, in the reach of its meaning, is higher than heaven and deeper than hell. Around it the New Testament is built. We do not find five, three, two, events, from which to select its natural centre. There is but one. Every other bends to that as a tributary. Take that out of the New Testament, and the significance of it is destroyed as hopelessly as that of the "Paradise Lost" would be if you eliminate the person of Satan.

A quality like that which science calls "aërial perspective" pervades the book, by which the light and shade of all other truths are magnified or reduced by their nearness or distance of relation to this one, — that a man whom other men understood to make himself the equal of God died an ignominious death on the cross. Even the letter of the volume hints at this. St. Matthew begins with, "The book of the generation of Jesus Christ; and St. John ends the vision of the Revelation with, "The grace of our Lord Jesus Christ be with you." The one image which fills up the whole interval between is Jesus Christ. A hungering, thirsting, suffering, praying, dying, buried, rising, ascending, interceding, reigning, exultant, and triumphant Redeemer, is the one burden of the story.

This concentration of biblical thought in the person of Christ is intensified further by *the biblical doctrine of the deity of Christ.* About this the Bible does not philosophize. It is presented as a simple *fact* in the biblical disclosure of Godhead. The Word was with God, and the Word was God. He is the brightness of the Father's glory, and the express image of his person. With such declarations the fact is left in its mysterious and sublime simplicity.

Men often ask us why we make so much of Christ in our religious life. Why magnify so loftily the name of Jesus? Was he not a Nazarene? Was he not born of a woman? Was he not the son of Joseph? Did not a carpenter claim his filial service? A precocious child, a wise man, a teacher, an example, a good man, a martyr, a man of mysterious command of supernatural forces; all that is good and great and amiable and reverend, if you please: still, was he not a babe in Bethlehem? Was he not swathed in a manger? Did he not hunger? Did he not thirst? Did he not slumber? Did he not weep? Did he not confess his ignorance? Did he not die? Did not the grave claim him as its victim? Believe him, then, pity him, revere him, trust him, love him, obey him, stand in awe before the mystery of his being, if you will; but why worship him? Why pray to him? Why make so much of him as to exalt him to the ineffable and adorable Godhead? Why turn away from the forests and the oceans and the heavens, which speak so grandly of Him who made them, to seek your God in a dying man?

Our answer is prompt and plain. It is, that in this Man of sorrows, this despised, rejected, suffering, dying One, we discern a disclosure of God of which Nature, in her most magnificent attire, can give us not a hint or conjecture. We go to Nature with souls burdened by the consciousness of sin, and we get nothing from her that speaks to our condition. Both the silence and the speech of Nature send us away from her in despair.

What says the speech of Nature? We ask her to give peace to our troubled conscience; and she tells us how old the mountains are, and where are the birthplaces of the rivers and the springs of the sea. We entreat her to tell us how we can obtain forgiveness; and she discourses proudly to us of gigantic flora and fauna, the buried races before man was. We press the question, "How can man be just with God?"—and she shows us exultingly the bones of the mastodon, and guesses wisely at the skeleton of the ichthyosaurus. We beg to be taught what we must do to be saved; and she turns to her telescope, and measures for us exactly the mountains of the moon, and tells us that its diameter is two thousand one hundred and sixty miles. On bended knees we beseech of her to reveal to us who shall deliver us from the body of this death; and she puts a microscope into our hands, and asks us to count the teeming population of an oak-leaf, and to observe what a tempestuous ocean a drop of water is. We respond, "Not that, not that; but tell us, oh, tell us, before it is too late, how we shall escape the damnation of hell!" And she proceeds with arithmetical precision to count for us the four thousand facets in the eyes of a house-fly.

Alas! what shall we do? We turn away in despair: we go mourning many days for the wisdom that shall make us wise unto salvation. The depth saith, "It is not with me." The sea saith, "It is not in me."

"It cannot be gotten for gold; neither shall silver be weighed for the price thereof. The gold of Ophir, the precious onyx, the sapphire, the crystal, cannot equal it. No mention shall be made of coral or of pearls. The price of it is above rubies. Whence, then, cometh it? and where *is* the place of it?" We have heard poets say that

"Nature
Never did desert the child that loved her."

But we do not find it so. We find that Nature *does* desert one who inquires of her after a God who can purify from guilt. To every such inquiry we find her dumb.

When we get nothing from her speech, we interrogate her silence; and that we find more pitiless than the grave. The silence of the rocks, and the silence of the waters, and the silence of the skies, all speak to us of Law. They proclaim, as the secret policy of God's government, immutable, merciless, damning Law. Every hint that the silence of Nature gives to a scorpion conscience is charged and surcharged with irreversible and endless doom. Interpreted by Nature's silence, the worm dieth not. We see, that, if we suffer shipwreck, the waters drown us. If we are hemmed in by forest fires, the flames burn us. If we seek shelter under a tree from the storms of heaven, the lightning strikes us. If we taste a poisonous berry in the woods, disease consumes us. If we fall asleep amid the fumes of charcoal, we never wake again. If we give ourselves to strong drink, hell gapes upon us before the time. Above, around, below, within us, we find Law, Law, Law, — nothing but Law. Our very being is an incarnate Law. We find no hint of such a thing as escape from the vengeance of an outraged Law. When did ever a law of nature lift a foot, or tread more lightly, because a praying *man* lay prostrate under it? Talk to Law of your sins, ask *her* how you can be forgiven, and she laughs at your calamity, she mocks when your fear comes. Law, therefore, suggests an eternal retribution for eternal sin. Why not? If we are crushed and mangled under the avenging tread of Law in this world, why not in another? Who can tell us?

Therefore it is that we turn in our emergency to seek for some other disclosure of God, if haply we may find it. Why may we not believe that we *have* found it in this revelation of God in Christ? Here we find a God who *can* pardon sin. Herein is the love we need, that, while we were yet *sinners*, Christ died, and died for us. The mystery of the God-man, the man-God, does not balk us. Sin is itself an anomaly in the moral universe. The forgiveness of sin is an anomaly at which angelic wisdom may well stand aghast. At the spectacle of sin unpunished, thoughtful intelligence, the universe through, may well tremble for the stability of God's throne. Till now, so far as we know, it has been unheard of in the history of the intelligent creation. We should expect the method of forgiveness to be full of mystery inexplicable to finite wisdom. The mystery of Christ is just like God, in such an anomaly of his government. Enough for us is it that it meets our case. Here God does speak to our condition. He comes down to a level with us. He takes our polluted hand within his own. He offers to create in us a new heart. What more can we ask for? We do not haggle about the life-boat that comes to take us from a burning wreck because we cannot make a life-boat. We do not spurn the hand of the fireman who lifts us from a blazing window because we do not see how he got there. Suffice it that we can be saved. We believe, we trust, we rejoice with joy unspeakable. Therefore it is that this thought of God in Christ has become so dear to his

Church. Therefore it is, that, for almost a thousand years, the Church of every name, and in many lands, has been singing the refrain of her St. Bernard, —

> "O Jesus, King most wonderful!
> Thou conqueror renowned!
> Thou sweetness most ineffable,
> In whom all joys are found!"

And therefore it is that the Church of to-day sends back her response to the ages, without one jot or tittle of abatement from the ancient faith, —

> "*My* faith looks up to thee,
> Thou Lamb of Calvary."

The centring of biblical truth in the person of Christ receives another, and, if possible, a grander illustration, *in the biblical doctrine of Christ's mediatorial reign.* This is the special teaching of the text before us. It is but a hint of a more resplendent revelation, which runs through the whole history of redemption. This "Son of man" in the night visions of the prophet is he to whom "all power is given in heaven and on earth. God has highly exalted him. At his name every knee shall bow, of things in heaven, and things in earth, and things under the earth."

We are not alone, then, in the interest we feel in Christ. He is the centre of thought also to the whole universe of mind. His is the empire of the universe. Sympathy with his work here is felt in distant worlds. Principalities and powers in heavenly places stand in awe-struck study around this one spot where the mystery of redemption is unfolding. A strange gravitation draws them to this one globe above all others in inhabited space. Such is the impression which the biblical glimpses of other worlds leave upon us. This is known to the universe as the "world of the cross." Lost spirits know it as the "world of the cross." Ministering angels know it as the "world of the cross." We do not know that another such world exists within the bounds of creation. If demoniacal alliances are formed against it, to clutch it from the hands of its Redeemer, from holy worlds come spiritual re-enforcements in innumerable battalions to its rescue. Dr. Chalmers did no violence to the scriptural disclosures of the reign of Christ, when he represented the worlds of invisible being as pulsating and growing tremulous in sympathy with the conflicts of the cross. In the biblical story of redemption our atmosphere seems populous with spiritual legions, marching and countermarching at the bidding of the Captain of our salvation.

My space will not permit me to do more than to mention the fact that the concentration of revealed truth in the person of Christ is further indicated by *the biblical doctrine of the eternal union of our Lord with the redeemed in heaven.*

II. Let us now observe some of the practical

bearings of this pre-eminence of Christ's person and work upon Christian faith and character.

1. It has an obvious bearing upon *the proportion and perspective of truth in a Christian's belief.* A religious creed may be made up of truths, and yet not be truthful. It may be false in its proportions. It may be delusive in its perspective. Some truths may be inflated, other truths may be scrimped. The resultant creed may be a monstrosity of distortion. Yet, taking it in pieces, doctrine by doctrine, it may be that not a falsehood is affirmed, and not a truth is denied. In the old punishment by torture, life was often racked out of the body by the mere distortion of thews and sinews, yet not a bone was broken. So a system of Christian faith, made up of Christian elements alone, may be paralyzed as a practical working-power by the sheer loss of symmetry, without denying one truth, or affirming one falsehood.

This tendency to dislocation in religious belief finds its most effectual corrective in the view we have just considered. The first thing necessary to the construction of a geometric circle is to fix its centre. So in the adjustment of a biblical faith, truthfulness of proportion depends on possession of the right centre. That is presumptively the most truthful faith, therefore, which works into the experience of the believer most effectually the reality of the person and the work of Christ. The biblical perspective exalts Christ. So should the thought of a crucified Saviour be the regnant thought in all Christian belief.

Christ thus enthroned in the believer's faith has a marvellous power to rectify speculative vagaries. It is difficult for such a believer to go wrong in other elements of his faith. He is not easily made a slave of crotchets. This single conception of God in Christ is charged with a centripetal magnetism which holds in obedient circuit around it all other truths, as the sun holds the planets. Let this one truth become regnant in the soul, and all other truths fall into rank around it, and turn inward towards it, as metallic particles do when a magnet approaches them. The cross, the cross, the cross, — this is the burden of inspired wisdom, this is the creative and corrective force in all Christian theory of doctrine.

2. The centring of truth in the person of Christ should, furthermore, *impart to Christian experience a profound sense of the reality of God as a personal friend*. God in Christ is brought home to the believer in these two aspects of his being, — as a living person, and as a present friend. In redemption we have to do, not so much with a device of government, as with a personal Redeemer. Divines talk much of the *plan* of salvation. Believers speak rather of the living One, the chief among ten thousand. The object of redeeming love is not man, but men; not the

race, but the man, the woman, the child. The race, as distinct from the individual souls who compose the race, is a fiction of the schools. An intense personality characterizes the whole transaction by which the sinner becomes a child of God. A personal Redeemer reaches forth, and takes to himself the personal believer.

Our hymnology often penetrates our theology more profoundly than our creeds can. Hence it is that our choicest hymns of praise, those which the Church seizes upon by intuition, and learns quickly by heart, are many of them founded on this sense of the personal possession of a personal Saviour.

3. Another effect of the pre-eminence of Christ in Christian faith should naturally be *to render the friends of Christ objects of personal and profound affection.* Profound affinity between the followers of Christ is an inevitable sequence from profound faith in him as the centre of all faith. It is the instinct of a redeemed sinner to grasp the hand of every other redeemed sinner. To identify himself with Christ's Church; to be known as one on whom rest the vows of Christ; to be called by the name of Christ; to make the interests of Christ's friends his own interests; to be loyal to the Christian brotherhood, as to kindred blood, — these are spontaneous impulses to a child of God. Christians are his friends simply because they are Christ's friends.

This experience is not cautiously reasoned out: it is involuntary. A child of God no more asks whether it is reasonable than he asks whether it is reasonable to breathe. Spontaneously he says, "Wherever I see a fellow-sinner clinging to the cross of Christ, there I behold my father, my mother, my brother, my sister. They may be my inferiors in wealth, in culture, in social rank: still they are my kindred. They may be of a weaker race, and of a despised complexion. The weight of the world's scorn, which centuries have accumulated, may be upon them. Still they are my kinsmen. They have been bought with a price, as I have been. My salvation is of no more value than theirs. It has cost no more: it is worth no more. I fill no larger space in the universe, as Christ regards it, any more than I shall fill a more gorgeous grave, or moulder back to dust in more magnificent or beautiful decay. Oh, no, no! The thing which distinguishes us all is, that Christ has chosen us. This it is which attracts to us the wondering gaze of spectators in distant worlds. This it is which surrounds us with a great cloud of witnesses. This is the crown of our glory, — that the Lamb of God has died for us, and the blood of sprinkling has been shed for us.

4. It follows, also, from the concentration of faith in the person of our Lord, *that the chief object of a regenerated life should be the object for which*

Christ lived and died. The genius of Christian living in this world is not mere philanthropy. It looks beyond and above the objects of philanthropic reform. It seeks that for which Christ died. No Christian life is true to itself which is not in this respect one with Christ's life. Philanthropy may be very well so far as it goes, but it is not necessarily Christian living.

The reason why religion and reform so often drift asunder is not that religion does not sympathize with reform, but that reform does not sympathize with religion. Reform plants itself on the temporal and earthly plane of benevolent working, and then claims that religion shall come down and work with it. Religion can only answer, "I cannot come down. Mine is the profounder reach into the heart of human woes; mine is the more radical method of their remedy. Come thou up, rather, and work with me." The object for which Christ lived, the methods of his procedure, the spirit of his dying words, — these are the model of a Christian manhood to every follower of Christ whose eye has not been hoodwinked in its perceptions of Christian duty and of Christian privilege.

5. The ascendency of Christ in Christian faith *gives character to a Christian's anticipations of heaven.* A system of religion may always be tested by its theory of the rewards of virtue in another life. The old mythologies told what they

were in the picture of Elysian fields. Islam proclaims its nature in its promise of a sensual paradise. The Scandinavian faith has its Valhalla. The North-American Indian has his happy hunting-grounds. Last and least of all, poetry and romance disclose their effeminacy in the doctrine of a "spirit land," of which nobody knows the character. The Christian heaven is distinguished from them all by this one peculiarity, — that Christ is there. There as here, Christ is the centre of holy thought. Heaven needs no sun or moon: the Lamb is the light thereof.

The single idea of meeting Christ, therefore, is the chief thing that makes heaven attractive to Christian hope. This it is that makes heaven our home. We are not qualified to go there till this thought does make it homelike to us. It is not the hope of happiness as such. It is not the thought of meeting patriarchs and prophets and apostles. It is not the hope of becoming the companions of heroic men who have suffered for the truth. It is not the prospect of sitting at the feet of Christian scholars, who may be still pursuing the researches in which they once fascinated us here. It is not the anticipation of meeting our favorite characters in history; the authors who have instructed us; the poets who have charmed us; the statesmen who have roused us to patriotic deeds; the preachers who have moved us by words which we expect to remember there; the writers of our favorite hymns, which we hope to have sung to us on our death-beds; men and women of the past, for whose creation we shall thank God forever, — it is not chiefly the hope of meeting this noble company that renders heaven attractive to Christian faith.

Nor is it the dearer hope of meeting our kindred there, of breaking the long silence of their graves, and hearing again loved voices, and seeing loved faces, and grasping loving hands again. No: not this is the central and regnant thought of heaven, when we seem to draw nearest to it, and to catch the reflection of its radiance on the hills, or to hear the echo of its strains in the midnight air. The thought which then entrances us is simply that Christ is there. " I shall see Christ. These eyes shall behold him. I, and not another. I shall be fitted to look upon him without shame. I shall be so changed that I can bear the look of his pure eye. I shall be able to stand erect in his presence. I shall have a crown to cast at his feet. He will own me as his friend. I shall reign with him. What that may mean, I do not know, but he knows, and that suffices. I shall be *satisfied* when I awake."

Such has been the thought of confessors of our faith in all ages, as they drew near the confines of that world. Martyrs, from St. Stephen downward, have rejoiced in this vision. When one of the most learned of the archbishops of England was on his death-bed, and friends sought to comfort him by a review of his great and noble life, said he, "Tell me not now of what I have done, or of what I have been. Tell me of Jesus Christ. I am going to meet him, my Lord and my God." Another of England's sainted ones, well known in her annals of Christian martyrdom, when the flames wreathed themselves around his form, seemed to see heaven opened; and he could tell what he saw there only in words of rapture: "None but Christ! none but Christ!"

OUR OTHER TITLE BY AUSTIN PHELPS

THE STILL HOUR

Austin Phelps (1820-1890) was a congregational minister, a professor of sacred rhetoric and homiletics, and later a president of Andover Theological Seminary. He wrote several books which were widely read, but none as much as *The Still Hour*. Some of the subjects covered are quite unique, such as "Absence of God, in Prayer", "Unhallowed Prayer", "Distrust in Prayer", "Indolence in Prayer" and "Idolatry in Prayer." This is a book that will both convict and encourage. It is perfect alike for the new believer and the aged saint who has walked with Christ for decades.

"Comforting, convicting, and correcting, Phelps's *Still Hour* is the best short book a Christian can read to stir up his or her sluggish soul and lay hold of God afresh by means of biblical, heartfelt prayer." - Joel R. Beeke

www.solid-ground-books.com
205-443-0311

OTHER TITLES FROM SOLID GROUND BOOKS

In addition to *Studies of the Old Testament*, Solid Ground Christian Books is honored to offer many other titles, many for the first time in more than a century:

THE MOTHER AT HOME by John S.C. Abbott
THE CHILD AT HOME by John S.C. Abbott
THE FAMILY AT HOME by Gorham Abbott
PUBLICATIONS OF THE AMERICAN TRACT SOCIETY
BIBLE PROMISES: *Sermons for Children* by Richard Newton
BIBLE WARNINGS: *Sermons for Children* by Richard Newton
BIBLE ANIMALS: *Lessons for the Children* by Richard Newton
BIBLE JEWELS: *Lessons for the Children* by Richard Newton
THE KING'S HIGHWAY: *10 Commandments for the Young* by R. Newton
HEROES OF THE REFORMATION by Richard Newton
HEROES OF THE EARLY CHURCH by Richard Newton
SAFE COMPASS AND HOW IT POINTS by Richard Newton
RAYS FROM THE SON OF RIGHTEOUSNESS by R. Newton
THE ASSURANCE OF FAITH *by Louis Berkhof*
THE PASTOR IN THE SICK ROOM *by John D. Wells*
THE LORD OF GLORY *by B.B. Warfield*
SERMONS TO THE NATURAL MAN *by W.G.T. Shedd*
SERMONS TO THE SPIRITUAL MAN *by W.G.T. Shedd*
A PASTOR'S SKETCHES 1 & 2 *by Ichabod S. Spencer*

Call us 205-443-0311
Send us an e-mail at mike.sgcb@gmail.com
Visit us on line at www.solid-ground-books.com